60 Soup Recipes for Home

By: Kelly Johnson

Table of Contents

- Classic Chicken Noodle Soup
- Creamy Tomato Basil Soup
- Minestrone Soup
- Broccoli Cheddar Soup
- Butternut Squash Soup
- French Onion Soup
- Lentil Soup
- Clam Chowder
- Potato Leek Soup
- Split Pea Soup
- Beef and Barley Soup
- Chicken Tortilla Soup
- Gazpacho
- Thai Tom Yum Soup
- Mushroom Soup
- Italian Wedding Soup
- Spinach and Lentil Soup
- Corn Chowder
- Moroccan Harira Soup
- Chicken and Rice Soup
- Avgolemono (Greek Lemon Chicken Soup)
- Pumpkin Soup
- Tortellini Soup
- Cuban Black Bean Soup
- Chicken and Dumplings Soup
- Roasted Red Pepper Soup
- Turkey Chili
- Ramen Noodle Soup
- Shrimp Bisque
- Sweet Potato and Coconut Soup
- Wonton Soup
- Creamy Cauliflower Soup
- Beef Stroganoff Soup
- White Bean and Kale Soup
- Sausage and Kale Soup

- Chicken Gumbo
- Matzo Ball Soup
- Acorn Squash Soup
- Vietnamese Pho
- Cabbage Roll Soup
- Wild Rice and Mushroom Soup
- Mexican Pozole
- New England Clam Chowder
- Lemon Chicken Orzo Soup
- Cucumber Avocado Soup
- Black-Eyed Pea Soup
- Italian Sausage and Bean Soup
- Pistou Soup
- Chicken and Corn Chowder
- White Gazpacho
- Zuppa Toscana
- Turkey and Wild Rice Soup
- Spicy Pumpkin Soup
- Artichoke Soup
- Chicken Mulligatawny Soup
- Chickpea and Spinach Soup
- Smoky Lentil Soup
- Creamy Asparagus Soup
- Beef Pho
- Lemon Dill Chicken Soup

Classic Chicken Noodle Soup

Ingredients:

- 1 tablespoon olive oil
- 1 onion, diced
- 2 carrots, sliced
- 2 celery stalks, sliced
- 3 cloves garlic, minced
- 1 teaspoon dried thyme
- 1 teaspoon dried rosemary
- 8 cups chicken broth
- 2 cups cooked chicken, shredded or diced
- 2 cups egg noodles
- Salt and black pepper to taste
- Fresh parsley, chopped, for garnish

Instructions:

In a large pot, heat olive oil over medium heat. Add diced onion, sliced carrots, and sliced celery. Cook until the vegetables are softened, about 5 minutes.
Add minced garlic, dried thyme, and dried rosemary to the pot. Cook for an additional 1-2 minutes until fragrant.
Pour in the chicken broth and bring the mixture to a simmer.
Add the cooked chicken to the pot and continue to simmer for about 10-15 minutes to allow the flavors to meld.
Meanwhile, in a separate pot, cook the egg noodles according to the package instructions. Drain and set aside.
Add the cooked egg noodles to the chicken soup and stir to combine.
Season the soup with salt and black pepper to taste. Adjust the seasoning if needed.
Simmer for an additional 5 minutes until the noodles are heated through.
Ladle the Classic Chicken Noodle Soup into bowls.
Garnish with chopped fresh parsley.
Serve the soup hot.

Enjoy this comforting and timeless Classic Chicken Noodle Soup for a warm and nourishing meal!

Creamy Tomato Basil Soup

Ingredients:

- 2 tablespoons olive oil
- 1 onion, chopped
- 2 cloves garlic, minced
- 2 cans (28 ounces each) whole tomatoes, undrained
- 1 can (14 ounces) diced tomatoes, undrained
- 1/4 cup tomato paste
- 1 cup vegetable or chicken broth
- 1 teaspoon sugar
- 1 teaspoon dried basil
- 1/2 teaspoon dried oregano
- 1/2 teaspoon salt (or to taste)
- 1/4 teaspoon black pepper (or to taste)
- 1 cup heavy cream
- Fresh basil leaves, for garnish (optional)
- Grated Parmesan cheese, for serving (optional)

Instructions:

In a large pot, heat olive oil over medium heat. Add chopped onion and sauté until softened, about 5 minutes.

Add minced garlic to the pot and cook for an additional 1-2 minutes until fragrant.

Add the whole tomatoes, diced tomatoes, and tomato paste to the pot. Break up the whole tomatoes using a spoon.

Pour in the vegetable or chicken broth, stirring to combine.

Add sugar, dried basil, dried oregano, salt, and black pepper to the pot. Stir well.

Bring the soup to a simmer, then reduce the heat to low. Cover and let it simmer for about 15-20 minutes to allow the flavors to meld.

Use an immersion blender to puree the soup until smooth. Alternatively, carefully transfer the soup in batches to a blender and blend until smooth. Be cautious with hot liquids.

Return the soup to the pot and stir in the heavy cream. Simmer for an additional 5-10 minutes.

Adjust the seasoning if needed.

Ladle the Creamy Tomato Basil Soup into bowls.

Garnish with fresh basil leaves and grated Parmesan cheese if desired.
Serve the soup hot, accompanied by crusty bread or croutons.

Enjoy this rich and velvety Creamy Tomato Basil Soup for a comforting and delicious meal!

Minestrone Soup

Ingredients:

- 2 tablespoons olive oil
- 1 onion, finely chopped
- 2 carrots, diced
- 2 celery stalks, diced
- 3 cloves garlic, minced
- 1 zucchini, diced
- 1 yellow squash, diced
- 1 cup green beans, cut into 1-inch pieces
- 1 can (14 ounces) diced tomatoes, undrained
- 1 can (15 ounces) kidney beans, drained and rinsed
- 1 can (15 ounces) cannellini beans, drained and rinsed
- 1 cup small pasta (e.g., ditalini or small shells)
- 8 cups vegetable or chicken broth
- 1 teaspoon dried oregano
- 1 teaspoon dried basil
- 1/2 teaspoon dried thyme
- Salt and black pepper to taste
- 2 cups spinach or kale, chopped
- Grated Parmesan cheese, for serving
- Fresh basil or parsley, chopped, for garnish

Instructions:

In a large pot, heat olive oil over medium heat. Add chopped onion, diced carrots, and diced celery. Cook until the vegetables are softened, about 5 minutes.
Add minced garlic to the pot and cook for an additional 1-2 minutes until fragrant.
Stir in diced zucchini, diced yellow squash, green beans, diced tomatoes, kidney beans, cannellini beans, and small pasta.
Pour in the vegetable or chicken broth and add dried oregano, dried basil, dried thyme, salt, and black pepper. Stir well.
Bring the soup to a simmer, then reduce the heat to low. Cover and let it simmer for about 15-20 minutes until the vegetables are tender.
Add chopped spinach or kale to the pot and simmer for an additional 5 minutes until wilted.

Adjust the seasoning if needed.
Ladle the Minestrone Soup into bowls.
Garnish with grated Parmesan cheese and chopped fresh basil or parsley.
Serve the soup hot, optionally with a side of crusty bread.

Enjoy this hearty and nutritious Minestrone Soup for a comforting and satisfying meal!

Broccoli Cheddar Soup

Ingredients:

- 1/4 cup unsalted butter
- 1 onion, chopped
- 2 carrots, peeled and diced
- 2 celery stalks, diced
- 3 cups broccoli florets
- 1/4 cup all-purpose flour
- 4 cups vegetable or chicken broth
- 2 cups milk
- 2 cups shredded sharp cheddar cheese
- Salt and black pepper to taste
- 1/4 teaspoon nutmeg (optional)
- 1/2 cup heavy cream (optional, for extra creaminess)
- Croutons, for garnish (optional)

Instructions:

In a large pot, melt butter over medium heat. Add chopped onion, diced carrots, and diced celery. Cook until the vegetables are softened, about 5 minutes.
Add broccoli florets to the pot and cook for an additional 3-5 minutes until slightly tender.
Stir in all-purpose flour, coating the vegetables evenly. Cook for 2-3 minutes to eliminate the raw flour taste.
Gradually pour in vegetable or chicken broth while stirring constantly to avoid lumps.
Add milk to the pot and continue to stir until the mixture thickens.
Using an immersion blender, blend the soup partially to achieve a chunky consistency. Alternatively, transfer a portion of the soup to a blender, blend, and return it to the pot.
Stir in shredded cheddar cheese until melted and smooth.
Season the soup with salt, black pepper, and nutmeg (if using). Adjust the seasoning to taste.
If desired, add heavy cream for extra creaminess.
Simmer the soup for an additional 10 minutes to allow the flavors to meld.
Ladle the Broccoli Cheddar Soup into bowls.
Garnish with croutons if desired.

Serve the soup hot, optionally with a side of crusty bread.

Enjoy this rich and comforting Broccoli Cheddar Soup for a warm and satisfying meal!

Butternut Squash Soup

Ingredients:

- 1 large butternut squash, peeled, seeded, and diced
- 2 tablespoons olive oil
- 1 onion, chopped
- 2 carrots, peeled and chopped
- 2 apples, peeled, cored, and chopped
- 4 cups vegetable or chicken broth
- 1 teaspoon ground cinnamon
- 1/2 teaspoon ground nutmeg
- 1/2 teaspoon ground ginger
- Salt and black pepper to taste
- 1 cup coconut milk or heavy cream
- 2 tablespoons maple syrup (optional, for sweetness)
- Toasted pumpkin seeds, for garnish (optional)
- Fresh parsley or chives, chopped, for garnish

Instructions:

Preheat the oven to 400°F (200°C).
Place the diced butternut squash on a baking sheet. Drizzle with olive oil and season with salt and black pepper. Toss to coat the squash evenly.
Roast the butternut squash in the preheated oven for about 25-30 minutes or until it is tender and slightly caramelized.
In a large pot, heat olive oil over medium heat. Add chopped onion, chopped carrots, and chopped apples. Cook until the vegetables are softened, about 5 minutes.
Add the roasted butternut squash to the pot.
Pour in the vegetable or chicken broth, ground cinnamon, ground nutmeg, and ground ginger. Stir well.
Bring the mixture to a simmer and let it cook for about 15-20 minutes to allow the flavors to meld.
Use an immersion blender to puree the soup until smooth. Alternatively, carefully transfer the soup in batches to a blender and blend until smooth. Be cautious with hot liquids.
Season the soup with salt and black pepper to taste.

Stir in coconut milk or heavy cream, and maple syrup if using. Simmer for an additional 5-10 minutes.
Adjust the seasoning and sweetness if needed.
Ladle the Butternut Squash Soup into bowls.
Garnish with toasted pumpkin seeds, chopped fresh parsley or chives.
Serve the soup hot, optionally with a drizzle of coconut milk or cream.

Enjoy this velvety and flavorful Butternut Squash Soup for a comforting and satisfying meal!

French Onion Soup

Ingredients:

- 4 large onions, thinly sliced
- 3 tablespoons unsalted butter
- 2 tablespoons olive oil
- 1 teaspoon sugar
- 4 cloves garlic, minced
- 1/2 cup dry white wine (optional)
- 4 cups beef broth
- 2 cups chicken broth
- 2 bay leaves
- 1 teaspoon dried thyme
- Salt and black pepper to taste
- Baguette slices
- 2 cups Gruyère cheese, grated

Instructions:

In a large pot, melt butter and olive oil over medium heat. Add the thinly sliced onions and sugar. Cook, stirring occasionally, for about 25-30 minutes or until the onions are deeply caramelized and golden brown.

Add minced garlic to the pot and cook for an additional 1-2 minutes until fragrant.

If using, pour in the dry white wine to deglaze the pot, scraping up any browned bits from the bottom.

Add beef broth, chicken broth, bay leaves, dried thyme, salt, and black pepper to the pot. Bring the mixture to a simmer and let it cook for an additional 15-20 minutes to allow the flavors to meld.

Preheat the oven broiler.

Meanwhile, arrange baguette slices on a baking sheet and toast them under the broiler for 1-2 minutes on each side or until they are golden brown.

Remove the bay leaves from the soup.

Ladle the French Onion Soup into oven-safe bowls.

Place a few toasted baguette slices on top of the soup.

Sprinkle a generous amount of grated Gruyère cheese over the bread slices, covering the surface.

Place the bowls under the broiler for 2-3 minutes or until the cheese is melted, bubbly, and golden brown.

Carefully remove the bowls from the oven.
Serve the French Onion Soup hot, being cautious of the hot bowls.

Enjoy this classic and comforting French Onion Soup with its rich flavors and cheesy topping!

Lentil Soup

Ingredients:

- 1 cup dried green or brown lentils, rinsed and drained
- 2 tablespoons olive oil
- 1 onion, chopped
- 2 carrots, diced
- 2 celery stalks, diced
- 3 cloves garlic, minced
- 1 teaspoon ground cumin
- 1 teaspoon ground coriander
- 1 teaspoon smoked paprika
- 1/2 teaspoon turmeric
- 1 bay leaf
- 6 cups vegetable or chicken broth
- 1 can (14 ounces) diced tomatoes, undrained
- 1 cup spinach or kale, chopped
- Juice of 1 lemon
- Salt and black pepper to taste
- Fresh parsley, chopped, for garnish

Instructions:

In a large pot, heat olive oil over medium heat. Add chopped onion, diced carrots, and diced celery. Cook until the vegetables are softened, about 5 minutes.

Add minced garlic to the pot and cook for an additional 1-2 minutes until fragrant.

Stir in ground cumin, ground coriander, smoked paprika, turmeric, and the bay leaf. Cook for 2-3 minutes to toast the spices.

Add rinsed lentils to the pot and stir to coat them in the spices.

Pour in vegetable or chicken broth and add diced tomatoes with their juice. Bring the mixture to a simmer.

Reduce the heat to low, cover the pot, and let it simmer for about 25-30 minutes or until the lentils are tender.

Stir in chopped spinach or kale and lemon juice. Simmer for an additional 5 minutes.

Season the Lentil Soup with salt and black pepper to taste. Adjust the seasoning if needed.

Remove the bay leaf from the soup.
Ladle the Lentil Soup into bowls.
Garnish with chopped fresh parsley.
Serve the soup hot, optionally with a drizzle of olive oil or a dollop of Greek yogurt.

Enjoy this wholesome and flavorful Lentil Soup for a nutritious and satisfying meal!

Clam Chowder

Ingredients:

- 4 slices bacon, chopped
- 1 onion, diced
- 2 celery stalks, diced
- 3 tablespoons all-purpose flour
- 3 cups potatoes, peeled and diced
- 2 cups vegetable or chicken broth
- 2 cups milk
- 2 cans (6.5 ounces each) chopped clams, undrained
- 1 bay leaf
- 1/2 teaspoon dried thyme
- Salt and black pepper to taste
- 1 cup heavy cream
- Fresh parsley, chopped, for garnish
- Oyster crackers, for serving (optional)

Instructions:

In a large pot, cook the chopped bacon over medium heat until it becomes crispy. Remove some of the bacon bits for garnish and leave some in the pot for flavor.
Add diced onion and diced celery to the pot with the bacon. Cook until the vegetables are softened, about 5 minutes.
Stir in all-purpose flour to create a roux, cooking for an additional 2-3 minutes.
Add diced potatoes to the pot.
Pour in vegetable or chicken broth and milk. Stir well to combine.
Add chopped clams with their juice, bay leaf, dried thyme, salt, and black pepper to the pot. Stir to combine.
Bring the mixture to a simmer, then reduce the heat to low. Cover and let it simmer for about 15-20 minutes or until the potatoes are tender.
Stir in heavy cream and simmer for an additional 5 minutes.
Remove the bay leaf from the chowder.
Adjust the seasoning if needed.
Ladle the Clam Chowder into bowls.
Garnish with the reserved bacon bits and chopped fresh parsley.
Serve the chowder hot, optionally with oyster crackers on the side.

Enjoy this rich and comforting Clam Chowder for a delicious and satisfying soup!

Potato Leek Soup

Ingredients:

- 3 leeks, white and light green parts, sliced
- 3 tablespoons unsalted butter
- 3 large potatoes, peeled and diced
- 4 cups vegetable or chicken broth
- 1 bay leaf
- 1 teaspoon dried thyme
- Salt and black pepper to taste
- 1 cup whole milk or heavy cream
- Fresh chives, chopped, for garnish (optional)
- Croutons or crusty bread, for serving

Instructions:

Clean the leeks thoroughly, as they can be sandy. Slice the leeks into thin rounds. In a large pot, melt the butter over medium heat. Add the sliced leeks and cook until they are softened, about 5 minutes.
Add the diced potatoes to the pot and stir to coat them in the butter and leeks. Pour in the vegetable or chicken broth. Add the bay leaf, dried thyme, salt, and black pepper. Stir well.
Bring the mixture to a simmer, then reduce the heat to low. Cover and let it simmer for about 15-20 minutes or until the potatoes are tender.
Remove the bay leaf from the soup.
Use an immersion blender to puree the soup until smooth. Alternatively, transfer a portion of the soup to a blender and blend until smooth. Be cautious with hot liquids.
Stir in whole milk or heavy cream, and simmer for an additional 5 minutes.
Adjust the seasoning if needed.
Ladle the Potato Leek Soup into bowls.
Garnish with chopped fresh chives if desired.
Serve the soup hot, optionally with croutons or crusty bread on the side.

Enjoy this creamy and comforting Potato Leek Soup for a delicious and warming meal!

Split Pea Soup

Ingredients:

- 1 pound (about 2 cups) dried split green peas, rinsed and sorted
- 1 ham hock or ham bone with some meat
- 1 onion, chopped
- 2 carrots, diced
- 2 celery stalks, diced
- 3 cloves garlic, minced
- 8 cups vegetable or chicken broth
- 1 bay leaf
- 1 teaspoon dried thyme
- Salt and black pepper to taste
- 1 cup ham, diced (if not using ham hock)
- 1 tablespoon olive oil (optional, for garnish)
- Fresh parsley, chopped, for garnish

Instructions:

In a large pot, combine the dried split peas, ham hock or ham bone, chopped onion, diced carrots, diced celery, minced garlic, vegetable or chicken broth, bay leaf, dried thyme, salt, and black pepper.
Bring the mixture to a boil, then reduce the heat to low. Cover and let it simmer for about 1 to 1.5 hours, or until the split peas are tender. Stir occasionally.
If using a ham hock, remove it from the pot and separate the meat from the bone. Dice the ham and return it to the pot. If using a ham bone, ensure any meat on the bone is diced and returned to the pot.
Remove the bay leaf from the soup.
Adjust the seasoning with additional salt and pepper if needed.
Optional: For a smoother consistency, use an immersion blender to partially puree the soup.
In a small pan, heat olive oil over medium heat. Add fresh parsley and sauté for a minute until fragrant. Drizzle this mixture over the soup as a garnish.
Ladle the Split Pea Soup into bowls.
Serve the soup hot, optionally with crusty bread on the side.

Enjoy this hearty and nutritious Split Pea Soup for a comforting and satisfying meal!

Beef and Barley Soup

Ingredients:

- 1 pound stew beef, cubed
- 2 tablespoons olive oil
- 1 onion, diced
- 2 carrots, diced
- 2 celery stalks, diced
- 3 cloves garlic, minced
- 1 cup pearl barley, rinsed
- 8 cups beef broth
- 1 can (14 ounces) diced tomatoes, undrained
- 1 bay leaf
- 1 teaspoon dried thyme
- Salt and black pepper to taste
- 1 cup frozen peas
- Fresh parsley, chopped, for garnish

Instructions:

In a large pot, heat olive oil over medium-high heat. Add cubed stew beef and brown on all sides.
Add diced onion, diced carrots, and diced celery to the pot. Cook until the vegetables are softened, about 5 minutes.
Stir in minced garlic and cook for an additional 1-2 minutes until fragrant.
Add rinsed pearl barley to the pot and stir to combine.
Pour in beef broth, diced tomatoes with their juice, bay leaf, dried thyme, salt, and black pepper. Stir well.
Bring the mixture to a simmer, then reduce the heat to low. Cover and let it simmer for about 45-60 minutes or until the beef is tender and the barley is cooked.
Remove the bay leaf from the soup.
Stir in frozen peas and cook for an additional 5 minutes.
Adjust the seasoning if needed.
Ladle the Beef and Barley Soup into bowls.
Garnish with chopped fresh parsley.
Serve the soup hot, optionally with crusty bread on the side.

Enjoy this hearty and flavorful Beef and Barley Soup for a satisfying and comforting meal!

Chicken Tortilla Soup

Ingredients:

- 1 pound boneless, skinless chicken breasts, cooked and shredded
- 2 tablespoons olive oil
- 1 onion, diced
- 3 cloves garlic, minced
- 1 jalapeño, seeded and diced (optional, for heat)
- 1 red bell pepper, diced
- 1 teaspoon ground cumin
- 1 teaspoon chili powder
- 1 teaspoon smoked paprika
- 1 can (14 ounces) diced tomatoes, undrained
- 1 can (4 ounces) diced green chilies
- 8 cups chicken broth
- 1 cup corn kernels (fresh, frozen, or canned)
- 1 can (15 ounces) black beans, drained and rinsed
- Salt and black pepper to taste
- Juice of 1 lime
- Fresh cilantro, chopped, for garnish
- Avocado slices, for garnish
- Shredded cheese, for garnish
- Tortilla strips or crushed tortilla chips, for topping

Instructions:

In a large pot, heat olive oil over medium heat. Add diced onion, minced garlic, diced jalapeño (if using), and diced red bell pepper. Cook until the vegetables are softened, about 5 minutes.

Stir in ground cumin, chili powder, and smoked paprika. Cook for an additional 2-3 minutes to toast the spices.

Add shredded cooked chicken to the pot and toss to combine with the vegetables and spices.

Pour in diced tomatoes, diced green chilies, and chicken broth. Stir well.

Bring the mixture to a simmer and let it cook for about 15-20 minutes to allow the flavors to meld.

Add corn kernels and black beans to the pot. Continue to simmer for an additional 10 minutes.

Season the Chicken Tortilla Soup with salt, black pepper, and lime juice. Adjust the seasoning if needed.
Ladle the soup into bowls.
Garnish with chopped fresh cilantro, avocado slices, shredded cheese, and tortilla strips or crushed tortilla chips.
Serve the soup hot.

Enjoy this zesty and comforting Chicken Tortilla Soup for a delicious and satisfying meal!

Gazpacho

Ingredients:

- 6 ripe tomatoes, cored and chopped
- 1 cucumber, peeled and diced
- 1 red bell pepper, seeded and chopped
- 1 green bell pepper, seeded and chopped
- 1 small red onion, chopped
- 3 cloves garlic, minced
- 4 cups tomato juice
- 1/4 cup red wine vinegar
- 1/4 cup olive oil
- 1 teaspoon salt (or to taste)
- 1/2 teaspoon black pepper (or to taste)
- 1 teaspoon sugar (optional, to balance acidity)
- 1 teaspoon Worcestershire sauce (optional)
- 1/4 teaspoon hot sauce (optional, for heat)
- Fresh basil or cilantro, chopped, for garnish
- Croutons, for serving (optional)

Instructions:

In a blender or food processor, combine chopped tomatoes, diced cucumber, chopped red and green bell peppers, chopped red onion, and minced garlic. Pulse until the vegetables are finely chopped but still have some texture.
Transfer the blended mixture to a large bowl.
Add tomato juice, red wine vinegar, olive oil, salt, black pepper, sugar (if using), Worcestershire sauce (if using), and hot sauce (if using). Stir well to combine.
Cover the bowl and refrigerate the Gazpacho for at least 2 hours or until it is well chilled.
Before serving, taste and adjust the seasoning if needed.
Ladle the Gazpacho into bowls.
Garnish with chopped fresh basil or cilantro.
Optionally, serve the Gazpacho with croutons on the side.

Enjoy this cool and refreshing Gazpacho as a delightful appetizer or light meal on a warm day!

Thai Tom Yum Soup

Ingredients:

- 4 cups chicken or vegetable broth
- 1 stalk lemongrass, cut into 2-inch pieces and smashed
- 3-4 kaffir lime leaves, torn into pieces
- 1-2 Thai bird's eye chilies, smashed (adjust for spice preference)
- 200g (7 oz) shrimp, peeled and deveined
- 200g (7 oz) mushrooms, sliced
- 1 medium tomato, cut into wedges
- 1 small onion, thinly sliced
- 2 tablespoons fish sauce
- 1 tablespoon soy sauce
- 1 tablespoon lime juice
- 1 teaspoon sugar
- Fresh cilantro leaves, for garnish
- Thai basil leaves, for garnish
- Sliced red chilies, for garnish

Instructions:

In a pot, bring the chicken or vegetable broth to a simmer.
Add smashed lemongrass, torn kaffir lime leaves, and smashed Thai bird's eye chilies to the pot. Let it simmer for about 5-10 minutes to infuse the flavors.
Add sliced mushrooms, tomato wedges, and sliced onion to the pot. Simmer for another 5 minutes until the vegetables are tender.
Stir in peeled and deveined shrimp, fish sauce, soy sauce, lime juice, and sugar. Cook until the shrimp turn pink and opaque, usually 3-5 minutes.
Taste the soup and adjust the seasoning if needed. You can add more fish sauce, lime juice, or sugar according to your preference.
Remove the lemongrass stalks and kaffir lime leaves from the soup.
Ladle the Tom Yum Soup into bowls.
Garnish with fresh cilantro leaves, Thai basil leaves, and sliced red chilies.
Serve the Tom Yum Soup hot, optionally with steamed jasmine rice on the side.

Enjoy this aromatic and flavorful Thai Tom Yum Soup for a delicious and comforting experience!

Mushroom Soup

Ingredients:

- 1 pound (about 500g) mushrooms, sliced (a mix of button mushrooms, cremini, and shiitake works well)
- 2 tablespoons unsalted butter
- 1 onion, finely chopped
- 2 cloves garlic, minced
- 4 cups vegetable or chicken broth
- 1 teaspoon thyme, dried or fresh
- Salt and black pepper to taste
- 1/4 cup all-purpose flour
- 1 cup milk or heavy cream
- Fresh parsley, chopped, for garnish (optional)

Instructions:

In a large pot, melt butter over medium heat. Add chopped onion and cook until it becomes translucent, about 5 minutes.
Add minced garlic to the pot and cook for an additional 1-2 minutes until fragrant.
Stir in sliced mushrooms and thyme. Cook until the mushrooms release their moisture and become golden brown.
Sprinkle flour over the mushroom mixture and stir well to coat. Cook for 2-3 minutes to eliminate the raw flour taste.
Gradually pour in vegetable or chicken broth while stirring constantly to avoid lumps.
Bring the soup to a simmer, then reduce the heat to low. Cover and let it simmer for about 15-20 minutes to allow the flavors to meld.
Use an immersion blender to partially puree the soup, leaving some mushroom pieces for texture. Alternatively, transfer a portion of the soup to a blender and blend until smooth. Be cautious with hot liquids.
Stir in milk or heavy cream and simmer for an additional 5 minutes.
Season the Mushroom Soup with salt and black pepper to taste. Adjust the seasoning if needed.
Ladle the soup into bowls.
Garnish with chopped fresh parsley if desired.
Serve the Mushroom Soup hot, optionally with crusty bread or croutons on the side.

Enjoy this rich and savory Mushroom Soup for a comforting and delicious meal!

Italian Wedding Soup

Ingredients:

For the Meatballs:

- 1/2 pound ground beef
- 1/2 pound ground pork
- 1/2 cup breadcrumbs
- 1/4 cup grated Parmesan cheese
- 1/4 cup chopped fresh parsley
- 1 clove garlic, minced
- 1 large egg
- Salt and black pepper to taste

For the Soup:

- 1 tablespoon olive oil
- 1 onion, finely chopped
- 2 carrots, diced
- 2 celery stalks, diced
- 2 cloves garlic, minced
- 8 cups chicken broth
- 1 bay leaf
- 1 teaspoon dried oregano
- 1 teaspoon dried thyme
- Salt and black pepper to taste
- 1 cup acini di pepe pasta or small pasta of your choice
- 4 cups fresh spinach or kale, chopped
- Grated Parmesan cheese, for serving

Instructions:

In a large mixing bowl, combine ground beef, ground pork, breadcrumbs, grated Parmesan cheese, chopped parsley, minced garlic, egg, salt, and black pepper. Mix until well combined.
Shape the mixture into small meatballs, about 1-inch in diameter.
In a large pot, heat olive oil over medium heat. Add chopped onion, diced carrots, and diced celery. Cook until the vegetables are softened, about 5 minutes.

Stir in minced garlic and cook for an additional 1-2 minutes until fragrant.
Pour in chicken broth, bay leaf, dried oregano, dried thyme, salt, and black pepper.
Bring the mixture to a simmer.
Gently drop the meatballs into the simmering broth and let them cook for about 10 minutes until cooked through.
Add acini di pepe pasta or your choice of small pasta to the pot and cook according to the package instructions until al dente.
Stir in chopped spinach or kale and cook for an additional 5 minutes until wilted.
Remove the bay leaf from the soup.
Adjust the seasoning if needed.
Ladle the Italian Wedding Soup into bowls.
Serve hot, garnished with grated Parmesan cheese.

Enjoy this comforting and hearty Italian Wedding Soup for a delicious and satisfying meal!

Spinach and Lentil Soup

Ingredients:

- 1 cup dried green or brown lentils, rinsed and drained
- 1 tablespoon olive oil
- 1 onion, chopped
- 2 carrots, diced
- 2 celery stalks, diced
- 3 cloves garlic, minced
- 1 teaspoon ground cumin
- 1 teaspoon ground coriander
- 1/2 teaspoon smoked paprika
- 6 cups vegetable or chicken broth
- 1 can (14 ounces) diced tomatoes, undrained
- 1 bay leaf
- Salt and black pepper to taste
- 4 cups fresh spinach, chopped
- Juice of 1 lemon
- Fresh parsley, chopped, for garnish
- Grated Parmesan cheese, for serving (optional)

Instructions:

In a large pot, heat olive oil over medium heat. Add chopped onion, diced carrots, and diced celery. Cook until the vegetables are softened, about 5 minutes.
Add minced garlic to the pot and cook for an additional 1-2 minutes until fragrant.
Stir in ground cumin, ground coriander, and smoked paprika. Cook for 2-3 minutes to toast the spices.
Add rinsed lentils to the pot and stir to coat them in the spices.
Pour in vegetable or chicken broth, diced tomatoes with their juice, and the bay leaf. Stir well.
Bring the mixture to a simmer and let it cook for about 25-30 minutes or until the lentils are tender.
Season the soup with salt and black pepper to taste.
Stir in chopped fresh spinach and lemon juice. Simmer for an additional 5 minutes until the spinach wilts.
Remove the bay leaf from the soup.
Adjust the seasoning if needed.

Ladle the Spinach and Lentil Soup into bowls.
Garnish with chopped fresh parsley.
Optionally, serve the soup hot with a sprinkle of grated Parmesan cheese on top.

Enjoy this nutritious and flavorful Spinach and Lentil Soup for a wholesome and satisfying meal!

Corn Chowder

Ingredients:

- 4 cups corn kernels (fresh, frozen, or canned)
- 4 slices bacon, chopped
- 1 onion, diced
- 2 celery stalks, diced
- 2 carrots, diced
- 3 potatoes, peeled and diced
- 4 cups chicken or vegetable broth
- 2 cups milk
- 1/4 cup all-purpose flour
- 1/2 teaspoon dried thyme
- Salt and black pepper to taste
- 1 cup heavy cream
- Fresh chives, chopped, for garnish (optional)
- Shredded cheddar cheese, for garnish (optional)

Instructions:

In a large pot, cook the chopped bacon over medium heat until it becomes crispy. Remove some of the bacon bits for garnish and leave some in the pot for flavor.
Add diced onion, diced celery, and diced carrots to the pot. Cook until the vegetables are softened, about 5 minutes.
Stir in peeled and diced potatoes and cook for an additional 3 minutes.
Sprinkle flour over the vegetable mixture and stir well to coat.
Pour in chicken or vegetable broth and add corn kernels. Stir to combine.
In a separate saucepan, heat milk until it's warm but not boiling.
Gradually whisk the warm milk into the pot with the vegetables and broth to avoid lumps.
Add dried thyme, salt, and black pepper to the chowder. Stir well.
Bring the chowder to a simmer and let it cook for about 15-20 minutes or until the potatoes are tender.
Stir in heavy cream and let the chowder simmer for an additional 5 minutes.
Adjust the seasoning if needed.
Ladle the Corn Chowder into bowls.
Garnish with chopped fresh chives and shredded cheddar cheese if desired.
Sprinkle the reserved bacon bits on top.

Serve the chowder hot, optionally with crusty bread or crackers on the side.

Enjoy this creamy and comforting Corn Chowder for a delicious and satisfying meal!

Moroccan Harira Soup

Ingredients:

- 1 cup dried chickpeas, soaked overnight and drained
- 1/2 cup green lentils, rinsed and drained
- 1/4 cup rice
- 2 tablespoons olive oil
- 1 onion, finely chopped
- 2 celery stalks, finely chopped
- 2 carrots, peeled and finely chopped
- 3 cloves garlic, minced
- 1 teaspoon ground cumin
- 1 teaspoon ground coriander
- 1 teaspoon ground cinnamon
- 1 teaspoon ground turmeric
- 1/2 teaspoon ground ginger
- 1/2 teaspoon paprika
- 1/4 teaspoon cayenne pepper (adjust to taste)
- 1 can (14 ounces) diced tomatoes, undrained
- 6 cups vegetable or chicken broth
- 1/2 cup fresh cilantro, chopped
- 1/2 cup fresh parsley, chopped
- Juice of 1 lemon
- Salt and black pepper to taste
- Hard-boiled eggs, chopped (for garnish, optional)
- Lemon wedges (for serving)
- Crusty bread or flatbread (for serving)

Instructions:

In a large pot, heat olive oil over medium heat. Add chopped onion, celery, and carrots. Cook until the vegetables are softened, about 5 minutes.

Add minced garlic to the pot and cook for an additional 1-2 minutes until fragrant. Stir in ground cumin, ground coriander, ground cinnamon, ground turmeric, ground ginger, paprika, and cayenne pepper. Cook for 2-3 minutes to toast the spices.

Add soaked and drained chickpeas, rinsed lentils, and rice to the pot. Stir to coat them in the spice mixture.

Pour in diced tomatoes with their juice and vegetable or chicken broth. Bring the mixture to a simmer.

Cover the pot and let it simmer for about 1 to 1.5 hours or until the chickpeas are tender.

Stir in chopped cilantro, chopped parsley, and lemon juice. Simmer for an additional 10-15 minutes.

Season the Harira Soup with salt and black pepper to taste. Adjust the seasoning if needed.

Ladle the soup into bowls.

Garnish with chopped hard-boiled eggs if desired.

Serve the Harira Soup hot, with lemon wedges on the side and crusty bread or flatbread for dipping.

Enjoy this hearty and flavorful Moroccan Harira Soup for a delicious and satisfying meal!

Chicken and Rice Soup

Ingredients:

- 1 tablespoon olive oil
- 1 onion, finely chopped
- 2 carrots, diced
- 2 celery stalks, diced
- 3 cloves garlic, minced
- 1 pound (about 500g) boneless, skinless chicken breasts, cut into small pieces
- 1 cup white rice, uncooked
- 8 cups chicken broth
- 1 teaspoon dried thyme
- 1 teaspoon dried rosemary
- Salt and black pepper to taste
- 1 bay leaf
- 1 cup frozen peas
- Fresh parsley, chopped, for garnish
- Lemon wedges, for serving

Instructions:

In a large pot, heat olive oil over medium heat. Add chopped onion, diced carrots, and diced celery. Cook until the vegetables are softened, about 5 minutes.
Add minced garlic to the pot and cook for an additional 1-2 minutes until fragrant.
Add cut chicken pieces to the pot and cook until they are no longer pink.
Stir in white rice and cook for 2-3 minutes to lightly toast the rice.
Pour in chicken broth and add dried thyme, dried rosemary, salt, black pepper, and the bay leaf. Stir well.
Bring the mixture to a simmer and let it cook for about 15-20 minutes or until the rice is cooked and the chicken is tender.
Add frozen peas to the pot and cook for an additional 5 minutes.
Remove the bay leaf from the soup.
Adjust the seasoning if needed.
Ladle the Chicken and Rice Soup into bowls.
Garnish with chopped fresh parsley.
Serve the soup hot, with lemon wedges on the side for squeezing.

Enjoy this comforting and wholesome Chicken and Rice Soup for a delicious and satisfying meal!

Avgolemono (Greek Lemon Chicken Soup)

Ingredients:

- 8 cups chicken broth
- 1/2 cup white rice
- 2 boneless, skinless chicken breasts, cooked and shredded
- 3 large eggs
- Juice of 2 lemons
- Salt and black pepper to taste
- Fresh dill, chopped, for garnish
- Lemon slices, for garnish

Instructions:

In a large pot, bring chicken broth to a simmer.
Add white rice to the pot and cook until it's tender, about 15-20 minutes.
Add shredded cooked chicken to the pot and stir to combine.
In a mixing bowl, whisk together eggs and lemon juice until well combined.
Gradually ladle about a cup of the hot broth into the egg-lemon mixture, whisking continuously to avoid curdling.
Slowly pour the egg-lemon mixture back into the pot, whisking constantly.
Continue to cook the soup over low heat, stirring gently, until it thickens slightly.
Be careful not to let it boil.
Season the Avgolemono with salt and black pepper to taste.
Remove the pot from heat.
Ladle the soup into bowls.
Garnish with chopped fresh dill and lemon slices.
Serve the Avgolemono Soup hot.

Enjoy this comforting and tangy Greek Lemon Chicken Soup for a delicious and warming meal!

Pumpkin Soup

Ingredients:

- 2 tablespoons olive oil
- 1 onion, chopped
- 2 cloves garlic, minced
- 1 teaspoon ground cumin
- 1/2 teaspoon ground coriander
- 1/2 teaspoon ground nutmeg
- 1/4 teaspoon cayenne pepper (optional, for heat)
- 4 cups pumpkin puree (canned or homemade)
- 4 cups vegetable or chicken broth
- 1 cup coconut milk
- Salt and black pepper to taste
- Pumpkin seeds, toasted, for garnish
- Fresh cilantro, chopped, for garnish
- Sour cream or yogurt, for garnish (optional)

Instructions:

In a large pot, heat olive oil over medium heat. Add chopped onion and cook until it becomes translucent, about 5 minutes.
Add minced garlic to the pot and cook for an additional 1-2 minutes until fragrant.
Stir in ground cumin, ground coriander, ground nutmeg, and cayenne pepper (if using). Cook for 2-3 minutes to toast the spices.
Add pumpkin puree and vegetable or chicken broth to the pot. Stir well to combine.
Bring the mixture to a simmer and let it cook for about 15-20 minutes to allow the flavors to meld.
Use an immersion blender to puree the soup until smooth. Alternatively, transfer the soup to a blender in batches and blend until smooth. Be cautious with hot liquids.
Stir in coconut milk and season the Pumpkin Soup with salt and black pepper to taste.
Simmer for an additional 5 minutes to heat through.
Adjust the seasoning if needed.
Ladle the soup into bowls.
Garnish with toasted pumpkin seeds and chopped fresh cilantro.

Optionally, add a dollop of sour cream or yogurt on top.
Serve the Pumpkin Soup hot.

Enjoy this creamy and flavorful Pumpkin Soup for a comforting and autumn-inspired meal!

Tortellini Soup

Ingredients:

- 1 tablespoon olive oil
- 1 onion, finely chopped
- 2 carrots, diced
- 2 celery stalks, diced
- 3 cloves garlic, minced
- 8 cups chicken or vegetable broth
- 1 can (14 ounces) diced tomatoes, undrained
- 1 teaspoon dried basil
- 1 teaspoon dried oregano
- 1/2 teaspoon dried thyme
- Salt and black pepper to taste
- 1 package (about 9 ounces) refrigerated cheese tortellini
- 2 cups fresh spinach or kale, chopped
- Grated Parmesan cheese, for serving
- Fresh basil, chopped, for garnish (optional)

Instructions:

In a large pot, heat olive oil over medium heat. Add chopped onion, diced carrots, and diced celery. Cook until the vegetables are softened, about 5 minutes.
Add minced garlic to the pot and cook for an additional 1-2 minutes until fragrant.
Pour in chicken or vegetable broth and add diced tomatoes with their juice. Stir well.
Add dried basil, dried oregano, dried thyme, salt, and black pepper to the pot. Bring the mixture to a simmer.
Once the soup is simmering, add the refrigerated cheese tortellini. Cook according to the package instructions until the tortellini are tender.
Stir in chopped fresh spinach or kale and cook for an additional 2-3 minutes until wilted.
Adjust the seasoning if needed.
Ladle the Tortellini Soup into bowls.
Serve hot, garnished with grated Parmesan cheese and chopped fresh basil if desired.

Enjoy this hearty and delicious Tortellini Soup for a satisfying and comforting meal!

Cuban Black Bean Soup

Ingredients:

- 2 cups dried black beans, soaked overnight and drained
- 2 tablespoons olive oil
- 1 onion, finely chopped
- 1 green bell pepper, diced
- 1 red bell pepper, diced
- 3 cloves garlic, minced
- 1 teaspoon ground cumin
- 1 teaspoon dried oregano
- 1/2 teaspoon ground coriander
- 1 bay leaf
- 6 cups vegetable or chicken broth
- 1 can (14 ounces) diced tomatoes, undrained
- Juice of 1 lime
- Salt and black pepper to taste
- Fresh cilantro, chopped, for garnish
- Sour cream or plain Greek yogurt, for garnish (optional)

Instructions:

In a large pot, heat olive oil over medium heat. Add chopped onion, diced green bell pepper, and diced red bell pepper. Cook until the vegetables are softened, about 5 minutes.

Add minced garlic to the pot and cook for an additional 1-2 minutes until fragrant. Stir in ground cumin, dried oregano, ground coriander, and the bay leaf. Cook for 2-3 minutes to toast the spices.

Add soaked and drained black beans, vegetable or chicken broth, and diced tomatoes with their juice to the pot. Stir well to combine.

Bring the mixture to a boil, then reduce the heat to low, cover, and simmer for about 1 to 1.5 hours or until the black beans are tender.

Remove the bay leaf from the soup.

Use an immersion blender to partially puree the soup, leaving some black beans for texture. Alternatively, transfer a portion of the soup to a blender and blend until smooth. Be cautious with hot liquids.

Stir in lime juice and season the Cuban Black Bean Soup with salt and black pepper to taste.

Adjust the seasoning if needed.
Ladle the soup into bowls.
Garnish with chopped fresh cilantro.
Optionally, add a dollop of sour cream or plain Greek yogurt on top.
Serve the Cuban Black Bean Soup hot.

Enjoy this flavorful and hearty Cuban Black Bean Soup for a delicious and satisfying meal!

Chicken and Dumplings Soup

Ingredients:

For the Soup:

- 1 tablespoon olive oil
- 1 onion, finely chopped
- 2 carrots, sliced
- 2 celery stalks, sliced
- 3 cloves garlic, minced
- 1 teaspoon dried thyme
- 1 teaspoon dried rosemary
- Salt and black pepper to taste
- 4 cups chicken broth
- 1 pound boneless, skinless chicken thighs, cut into bite-sized pieces
- 1 cup frozen peas
- 1 cup frozen corn
- 1 cup milk
- 1/2 cup all-purpose flour

For the Dumplings:

- 1 cup all-purpose flour
- 1 1/2 teaspoons baking powder
- 1/2 teaspoon salt
- 1/2 cup milk
- 2 tablespoons unsalted butter, melted

Instructions:

In a large pot, heat olive oil over medium heat. Add chopped onion, sliced carrots, and sliced celery. Cook until the vegetables are softened, about 5 minutes.
Add minced garlic, dried thyme, dried rosemary, salt, and black pepper to the pot. Cook for an additional 1-2 minutes until fragrant.
Pour in chicken broth and add bite-sized pieces of chicken to the pot. Bring the mixture to a simmer and let it cook for about 10-15 minutes until the chicken is cooked through.
Stir in frozen peas and frozen corn.

In a separate bowl, whisk together flour and milk until well combined and smooth. Pour the flour and milk mixture into the soup, stirring constantly to avoid lumps.

Continue to cook the soup until it thickens slightly.

In a separate bowl, mix together the ingredients for the dumplings: flour, baking powder, salt, milk, and melted butter. Stir until just combined.

Drop spoonfuls of the dumpling mixture onto the simmering soup. Cover the pot with a lid and let the dumplings cook for about 15-20 minutes until they are cooked through and have doubled in size.

Ladle the Chicken and Dumplings Soup into bowls.

Serve hot, and enjoy!

This comforting Chicken and Dumplings Soup is perfect for a cozy and satisfying meal!

Roasted Red Pepper Soup

Ingredients:

- 4 large red bell peppers, roasted, peeled, and chopped
- 2 tablespoons olive oil
- 1 onion, chopped
- 3 cloves garlic, minced
- 1 carrot, diced
- 1 celery stalk, diced
- 1 potato, peeled and diced
- 4 cups vegetable or chicken broth
- 1 can (14 ounces) diced tomatoes, undrained
- 1 teaspoon dried thyme
- Salt and black pepper to taste
- 1/2 cup heavy cream (optional, for creaminess)
- Fresh basil, chopped, for garnish
- Croutons or bread, for serving

Instructions:

Preheat the oven to broil. Place the red bell peppers on a baking sheet and broil, turning occasionally, until the skin is charred and blistered. Remove from the oven and place the peppers in a bowl, covering it with plastic wrap. Allow the peppers to cool, then peel, seed, and chop them.
In a large pot, heat olive oil over medium heat. Add chopped onion, minced garlic, diced carrot, diced celery, and diced potato. Cook until the vegetables are softened, about 5 minutes.
Add the roasted and chopped red bell peppers to the pot and stir to combine. Pour in vegetable or chicken broth, add diced tomatoes with their juice, and add dried thyme. Bring the mixture to a simmer.
Cover the pot and let it simmer for about 20-25 minutes or until the vegetables are tender.
Use an immersion blender to puree the soup until smooth. Alternatively, transfer the soup to a blender in batches and blend until smooth. Be cautious with hot liquids.
Season the Roasted Red Pepper Soup with salt and black pepper to taste.
If you prefer a creamy soup, stir in heavy cream and let it simmer for an additional 5 minutes.

Adjust the seasoning if needed.
Ladle the soup into bowls.
Garnish with chopped fresh basil.
Serve hot, optionally with croutons or crusty bread on the side.

Enjoy this flavorful and vibrant Roasted Red Pepper Soup for a delightful and comforting meal!

Turkey Chili

Ingredients:

- 1 tablespoon olive oil
- 1 onion, chopped
- 3 cloves garlic, minced
- 1 pound ground turkey
- 1 bell pepper, diced
- 1 jalapeño pepper, seeded and minced (optional, for heat)
- 1 can (14 ounces) diced tomatoes, undrained
- 1 can (15 ounces) kidney beans, drained and rinsed
- 1 can (15 ounces) black beans, drained and rinsed
- 1 cup corn kernels (fresh, frozen, or canned)
- 2 tablespoons tomato paste
- 1 cup chicken broth
- 2 teaspoons chili powder
- 1 teaspoon ground cumin
- 1 teaspoon smoked paprika
- 1/2 teaspoon dried oregano
- Salt and black pepper to taste
- 1 cup shredded cheddar cheese, for garnish
- Fresh cilantro, chopped, for garnish
- Sour cream, for serving (optional)
- Tortilla chips, for serving

Instructions:

In a large pot, heat olive oil over medium heat. Add chopped onion and cook until it becomes translucent, about 5 minutes.

Add minced garlic to the pot and cook for an additional 1-2 minutes until fragrant.

Add ground turkey to the pot and cook until it's browned, breaking it apart with a spoon.

Stir in diced bell pepper and minced jalapeño (if using) and cook for an additional 3-5 minutes.

Add diced tomatoes with their juice, kidney beans, black beans, corn, tomato paste, and chicken broth to the pot. Stir well to combine.

Season the turkey chili with chili powder, ground cumin, smoked paprika, dried oregano, salt, and black pepper. Stir to incorporate the spices.
Bring the mixture to a simmer, then reduce the heat to low. Cover and let it simmer for about 30-40 minutes to allow the flavors to meld.
Adjust the seasoning if needed.
Ladle the turkey chili into bowls.
Garnish with shredded cheddar cheese and chopped fresh cilantro.
Optionally, serve with a dollop of sour cream and tortilla chips on the side.

Enjoy this hearty and flavorful Turkey Chili for a delicious and satisfying meal!

Ramen Noodle Soup

Ingredients:

- 2 packs of instant ramen noodles (discard seasoning packets or use them if preferred)
- 1 tablespoon sesame oil
- 1 onion, thinly sliced
- 2 cloves garlic, minced
- 1-inch piece of ginger, grated
- 4 cups vegetable or chicken broth
- 1 tablespoon soy sauce
- 1 tablespoon miso paste (optional)
- 1 carrot, julienned
- 1 cup mushrooms, sliced
- 2 cups baby spinach
- 2 green onions, sliced
- Soft-boiled eggs, halved (optional, for serving)
- Nori seaweed, sliced (optional, for garnish)
- Sesame seeds, for garnish

Instructions:

Cook the instant ramen noodles according to the package instructions. Drain and set aside.
In a large pot, heat sesame oil over medium heat. Add thinly sliced onion, minced garlic, and grated ginger. Sauté until the onion becomes translucent, about 3-5 minutes.
Pour in vegetable or chicken broth and bring it to a simmer.
Add soy sauce and miso paste (if using) to the broth. Stir to dissolve the miso paste.
Add julienned carrot, sliced mushrooms, and cooked ramen noodles to the pot.
Simmer for an additional 5-7 minutes until the vegetables are tender.
Stir in baby spinach and cook until it wilts.
Adjust the seasoning by adding more soy sauce or miso paste if needed.
Ladle the Ramen Noodle Soup into bowls.
Garnish with sliced green onions, halved soft-boiled eggs, nori seaweed, and sesame seeds.

Serve hot and enjoy!

Feel free to customize your Ramen Noodle Soup by adding other ingredients like tofu, shredded chicken, or your favorite vegetables.

Shrimp Bisque

Ingredients:

- 1 pound shrimp, peeled and deveined
- 2 tablespoons olive oil
- 1 onion, chopped
- 2 carrots, chopped
- 2 celery stalks, chopped
- 3 cloves garlic, minced
- 1/4 cup tomato paste
- 1/4 cup all-purpose flour
- 4 cups seafood or vegetable broth
- 1 cup dry white wine
- 1 cup heavy cream
- 1 teaspoon paprika
- 1/2 teaspoon cayenne pepper (adjust to taste)
- Salt and black pepper to taste
- 2 tablespoons brandy (optional)
- Fresh parsley, chopped, for garnish
- Croutons or crusty bread, for serving

Instructions:

In a large pot, heat olive oil over medium heat. Add chopped onion, chopped carrots, and chopped celery. Cook until the vegetables are softened, about 5 minutes.

Add minced garlic to the pot and cook for an additional 1-2 minutes until fragrant.

Stir in tomato paste and cook for 2-3 minutes to enhance the flavor.

Sprinkle flour over the vegetables and stir well to create a roux.

Gradually pour in seafood or vegetable broth and dry white wine, stirring continuously to avoid lumps.

Add peeled and deveined shrimp to the pot. Let the mixture simmer for about 10-15 minutes until the shrimp are cooked through.

Use an immersion blender to puree the soup until smooth. Alternatively, transfer a portion of the soup to a blender and blend until smooth. Be cautious with hot liquids.

Stir in heavy cream, paprika, cayenne pepper, salt, and black pepper. Simmer for an additional 5-7 minutes.

Optionally, add brandy to the bisque for extra flavor.
Adjust the seasoning if needed.
Ladle the Shrimp Bisque into bowls.
Garnish with chopped fresh parsley.
Serve hot, optionally with croutons or crusty bread on the side.

Enjoy this rich and flavorful Shrimp Bisque for a delightful and elegant meal!

Sweet Potato and Coconut Soup

Ingredients:

- 2 tablespoons coconut oil
- 1 onion, chopped
- 3 cloves garlic, minced
- 2 teaspoons ginger, grated
- 3 large sweet potatoes, peeled and diced
- 1 can (14 ounces) coconut milk
- 4 cups vegetable broth
- 1 teaspoon curry powder
- 1/2 teaspoon ground cinnamon
- 1/4 teaspoon cayenne pepper (adjust to taste)
- Salt and black pepper to taste
- Juice of 1 lime
- Fresh cilantro, chopped, for garnish
- Toasted coconut flakes, for garnish

Instructions:

In a large pot, heat coconut oil over medium heat. Add chopped onion and cook until it becomes translucent, about 5 minutes.
Add minced garlic and grated ginger to the pot. Cook for an additional 1-2 minutes until fragrant.
Add diced sweet potatoes to the pot and stir to coat them in the aromatic mixture.
Pour in coconut milk and vegetable broth. Stir well to combine.
Add curry powder, ground cinnamon, cayenne pepper, salt, and black pepper. Stir to incorporate the spices.
Bring the mixture to a boil, then reduce the heat to low, cover, and let it simmer for about 20-25 minutes or until the sweet potatoes are tender.
Use an immersion blender to puree the soup until smooth. Alternatively, transfer a portion of the soup to a blender and blend until smooth. Be cautious with hot liquids.
Stir in lime juice and adjust the seasoning if needed.
Ladle the Sweet Potato and Coconut Soup into bowls.
Garnish with chopped fresh cilantro and toasted coconut flakes.

Serve hot and enjoy!

This Sweet Potato and Coconut Soup is creamy, comforting, and has a perfect blend of sweet and savory flavors.

Wonton Soup

Ingredients:

For the Wontons:

- 1/2 pound ground pork
- 1/2 pound raw shrimp, peeled, deveined, and finely chopped
- 2 green onions, finely chopped
- 1 tablespoon soy sauce
- 1 tablespoon oyster sauce
- 1 teaspoon sesame oil
- 1 teaspoon ginger, grated
- 1 teaspoon cornstarch
- Wonton wrappers

For the Soup:

- 8 cups chicken broth
- 2 cloves garlic, minced
- 1 tablespoon soy sauce
- 1 tablespoon sesame oil
- 2 cups bok choy or baby spinach, chopped
- 1 cup sliced mushrooms
- 1 carrot, julienned
- Green onions, sliced, for garnish

Instructions:

In a bowl, combine ground pork, chopped shrimp, green onions, soy sauce, oyster sauce, sesame oil, ginger, and cornstarch. Mix well to form the wonton filling. Place a small spoonful of the filling in the center of a wonton wrapper. Moisten the edges of the wrapper with water, then fold it in half to form a triangle. Press the edges to seal, making sure to remove any air pockets. Repeat until all wontons are assembled.

In a large pot, bring chicken broth to a simmer. Add minced garlic, soy sauce, and sesame oil.

Drop the wontons into the simmering broth and cook for about 5-7 minutes or until they float to the surface.

Add bok choy or baby spinach, sliced mushrooms, and julienned carrot to the soup. Cook for an additional 3-5 minutes until the vegetables are tender.

Adjust the seasoning if needed.

Ladle the Wonton Soup into bowls.

Garnish with sliced green onions.

Serve hot and enjoy!

This homemade Wonton Soup is comforting and filled with delicious flavors. Feel free to customize the soup with your favorite vegetables and enjoy this classic Chinese dish!

Creamy Cauliflower Soup

Ingredients:

- 1 large cauliflower, chopped into florets
- 1 onion, chopped
- 2 cloves garlic, minced
- 2 tablespoons olive oil
- 4 cups vegetable broth
- 1 cup whole milk or heavy cream
- 1 bay leaf
- 1 teaspoon dried thyme
- Salt and black pepper to taste
- Fresh chives, chopped, for garnish
- Grated Parmesan cheese, for garnish (optional)
- Croutons or crusty bread, for serving

Instructions:

In a large pot, heat olive oil over medium heat. Add chopped onion and cook until it becomes translucent, about 5 minutes.
Add minced garlic to the pot and cook for an additional 1-2 minutes until fragrant.
Add cauliflower florets to the pot and stir to coat them in the aromatic mixture.
Pour in vegetable broth, add a bay leaf, and bring the mixture to a simmer. Cook for about 15-20 minutes or until the cauliflower is tender.
Remove the bay leaf from the pot.
Use an immersion blender to puree the soup until smooth. Alternatively, transfer the soup to a blender in batches and blend until smooth. Be cautious with hot liquids.
Stir in whole milk or heavy cream and dried thyme. Simmer for an additional 5 minutes.
Season the Creamy Cauliflower Soup with salt and black pepper to taste.
Adjust the seasoning if needed.
Ladle the soup into bowls.
Garnish with chopped fresh chives and grated Parmesan cheese if desired.
Optionally, serve with croutons or crusty bread on the side.

Enjoy this velvety and satisfying Creamy Cauliflower Soup for a comforting and nutritious meal!

Beef Stroganoff Soup

Ingredients:

- 1 pound beef sirloin or tenderloin, thinly sliced
- 2 tablespoons olive oil
- 1 onion, finely chopped
- 2 cloves garlic, minced
- 8 ounces cremini or white mushrooms, sliced
- 3 tablespoons all-purpose flour
- 4 cups beef broth
- 1 tablespoon Worcestershire sauce
- 1 teaspoon Dijon mustard
- 1 teaspoon paprika
- Salt and black pepper to taste
- 1 cup egg noodles, uncooked
- 1 cup sour cream
- Fresh parsley, chopped, for garnish

Instructions:

In a large pot, heat olive oil over medium heat. Add thinly sliced beef and cook until browned. Remove the beef from the pot and set it aside.
In the same pot, add chopped onion and cook until it becomes translucent, about 5 minutes.
Add minced garlic to the pot and cook for an additional 1-2 minutes until fragrant.
Stir in sliced mushrooms and cook until they release their moisture and become golden brown.
Sprinkle flour over the mushroom mixture and stir well to create a roux.
Gradually pour in beef broth, Worcestershire sauce, Dijon mustard, paprika, salt, and black pepper. Stir to combine.
Add uncooked egg noodles to the pot. Simmer for about 8-10 minutes or until the noodles are tender.
Return the browned beef to the pot and let it simmer for an additional 5-7 minutes.
Stir in sour cream and let the soup heat through without boiling.
Adjust the seasoning if needed.
Ladle the Beef Stroganoff Soup into bowls.

Garnish with chopped fresh parsley.

Enjoy this hearty and flavorful Beef Stroganoff Soup for a comforting and satisfying meal!

White Bean and Kale Soup

Ingredients:

- 2 tablespoons olive oil
- 1 onion, chopped
- 2 carrots, diced
- 3 celery stalks, diced
- 3 cloves garlic, minced
- 1 teaspoon dried thyme
- 2 cans (15 ounces each) white beans, drained and rinsed
- 6 cups vegetable or chicken broth
- 1 bay leaf
- 1 bunch kale, stems removed and leaves chopped
- Salt and black pepper to taste
- 1 teaspoon lemon juice (optional, for brightness)
- Grated Parmesan cheese, for garnish
- Crusty bread, for serving

Instructions:

In a large pot, heat olive oil over medium heat. Add chopped onion, diced carrots, and diced celery. Cook until the vegetables are softened, about 5 minutes.
Add minced garlic and dried thyme to the pot. Cook for an additional 1-2 minutes until fragrant.
Stir in white beans, vegetable or chicken broth, and add a bay leaf. Bring the mixture to a simmer.
Add chopped kale to the pot and simmer for about 10-15 minutes until the kale is tender.
Season the White Bean and Kale Soup with salt and black pepper to taste.
Optionally, add lemon juice for a hint of brightness.
Remove the bay leaf from the soup.
Adjust the seasoning if needed.
Ladle the soup into bowls.
Garnish with grated Parmesan cheese.
Serve hot, optionally with crusty bread on the side.

Enjoy this nutritious and hearty White Bean and Kale Soup for a delicious and comforting meal!

Sausage and Kale Soup

Ingredients:

- 1 pound Italian sausage, casings removed
- 2 tablespoons olive oil
- 1 onion, chopped
- 3 cloves garlic, minced
- 2 carrots, sliced
- 3 potatoes, diced
- 1 teaspoon dried thyme
- 1 teaspoon dried rosemary
- 1 bay leaf
- 6 cups chicken or vegetable broth
- 1 bunch kale, stems removed and leaves chopped
- Salt and black pepper to taste
- Grated Parmesan cheese, for garnish
- Crushed red pepper flakes, for garnish (optional)
- Crusty bread, for serving

Instructions:

In a large pot, cook Italian sausage over medium heat, breaking it apart with a spoon, until browned and cooked through. Remove excess fat if necessary.
Add olive oil to the pot and add chopped onion. Cook until the onion is softened, about 5 minutes.
Add minced garlic to the pot and cook for an additional 1-2 minutes until fragrant.
Stir in sliced carrots, diced potatoes, dried thyme, dried rosemary, and the bay leaf. Cook for 3-5 minutes to allow the vegetables to absorb the flavors.
Pour in chicken or vegetable broth and bring the mixture to a simmer.
Add chopped kale to the pot and simmer for about 10-15 minutes until the kale is tender.
Season the Sausage and Kale Soup with salt and black pepper to taste.
Remove the bay leaf from the soup.
Adjust the seasoning if needed.
Ladle the soup into bowls.
Garnish with grated Parmesan cheese and crushed red pepper flakes if desired.
Serve hot, optionally with crusty bread on the side.

Enjoy this hearty and flavorful Sausage and Kale Soup for a comforting and satisfying meal!

Chicken Gumbo

Ingredients:

- 1/2 cup vegetable oil
- 1/2 cup all-purpose flour
- 1 onion, chopped
- 1 bell pepper, chopped
- 2 celery stalks, chopped
- 3 cloves garlic, minced
- 1 pound boneless, skinless chicken thighs, cut into bite-sized pieces
- 1 pound andouille sausage, sliced
- 1 can (14 ounces) diced tomatoes, undrained
- 4 cups chicken broth
- 1 bay leaf
- 1 teaspoon dried thyme
- 1 teaspoon dried oregano
- 1 teaspoon smoked paprika
- 1/2 teaspoon cayenne pepper (adjust to taste)
- Salt and black pepper to taste
- 1 cup okra, sliced (fresh or frozen)
- 1 cup sliced okra (fresh or frozen)
- 1 cup sliced green onions, for garnish
- Cooked white rice, for serving

Instructions:

In a large pot, make a roux by combining vegetable oil and flour over medium heat. Stir continuously until the roux reaches a dark brown color. Be careful not to burn it.

Add chopped onion, chopped bell pepper, chopped celery, and minced garlic to the roux. Cook for about 5 minutes until the vegetables are softened.

Add bite-sized pieces of chicken thighs and sliced andouille sausage to the pot. Cook until the chicken is browned.

Stir in diced tomatoes with their juice and chicken broth. Add a bay leaf, dried thyme, dried oregano, smoked paprika, cayenne pepper, salt, and black pepper. Stir to combine.

Bring the mixture to a simmer, then reduce the heat to low. Cover and let it simmer for about 30 minutes to allow the flavors to meld.
Add sliced okra to the pot and simmer for an additional 10-15 minutes until the okra is tender.
Adjust the seasoning if needed.
Remove the bay leaf from the Chicken Gumbo.
Ladle the gumbo into bowls.
Garnish with sliced green onions.
Serve hot over cooked white rice.

Enjoy this flavorful and hearty Chicken Gumbo for a taste of Creole cuisine!

Matzo Ball Soup

Ingredients:

For the Matzo Balls:

- 2/3 cup matzo meal
- 2 large eggs
- 2 tablespoons vegetable oil
- 2 tablespoons chicken broth or water
- 1/2 teaspoon salt
- 1/4 teaspoon black pepper
- 1/4 teaspoon baking powder

For the Soup:

- 8 cups chicken broth
- 2 carrots, sliced
- 2 celery stalks, sliced
- 1 onion, chopped
- 2 cloves garlic, minced
- 1 parsnip, sliced (optional)
- Fresh dill, chopped, for garnish
- Salt and black pepper to taste

Instructions:

For the Matzo Balls:

In a bowl, whisk together matzo meal, eggs, vegetable oil, chicken broth or water, salt, black pepper, and baking powder until well combined.
Cover the bowl and refrigerate the mixture for at least 30 minutes.
Bring a large pot of salted water to a simmer.
Wet your hands and form the matzo mixture into 1-inch balls. Drop the balls into the simmering water.
Cover the pot and let the matzo balls simmer for about 30-40 minutes until they are cooked through and fluffy.

Using a slotted spoon, transfer the matzo balls to a plate and set aside.

For the Soup:

In a large pot, bring chicken broth to a simmer.
Add sliced carrots, sliced celery, chopped onion, minced garlic, and sliced parsnip (if using) to the pot. Cook until the vegetables are tender, about 10-15 minutes.
Season the soup with salt and black pepper to taste.
Add the cooked matzo balls to the soup.
Ladle the Matzo Ball Soup into bowls.
Garnish with chopped fresh dill.
Serve hot and enjoy!

This classic Matzo Ball Soup is warm, comforting, and perfect for any occasion!

Acorn Squash Soup

Ingredients:

- 2 acorn squash, halved and seeds removed
- 2 tablespoons olive oil
- 1 onion, chopped
- 2 carrots, peeled and chopped
- 2 celery stalks, chopped
- 2 cloves garlic, minced
- 4 cups vegetable or chicken broth
- 1 teaspoon ground cinnamon
- 1/2 teaspoon ground nutmeg
- Salt and black pepper to taste
- 1 cup coconut milk or heavy cream
- Toasted pumpkin seeds, for garnish
- Fresh thyme, for garnish (optional)

Instructions:

Preheat the oven to 400°F (200°C).

Place the acorn squash halves, cut side up, on a baking sheet. Drizzle with olive oil and season with salt and black pepper.

Roast the acorn squash in the preheated oven for about 45-50 minutes or until the squash is tender and can be easily pierced with a fork.

Once the squash is roasted, let it cool slightly, then scoop out the flesh from the skins.

In a large pot, heat olive oil over medium heat. Add chopped onion, chopped carrots, chopped celery, and minced garlic. Cook until the vegetables are softened, about 5 minutes.

Add the roasted acorn squash flesh to the pot and stir to combine.

Pour in vegetable or chicken broth, ground cinnamon, and ground nutmeg. Bring the mixture to a simmer.

Use an immersion blender to puree the soup until smooth. Alternatively, transfer the soup to a blender in batches and blend until smooth. Be cautious with hot liquids.

Stir in coconut milk or heavy cream and let the soup simmer for an additional 5-7 minutes.

Season the Acorn Squash Soup with salt and black pepper to taste.

Adjust the seasoning if needed.
Ladle the soup into bowls.
Garnish with toasted pumpkin seeds and fresh thyme if desired.
Serve hot and enjoy!

This Acorn Squash Soup is creamy, flavorful, and perfect for a comforting meal.

Vietnamese Pho

Ingredients:

For the Broth:

- 2 large onions, halved
- 1 ginger piece (about 3 inches), sliced
- 3-4 lbs beef bones (mix of marrow and knuckle bones)
- 1 cinnamon stick
- 3 star anise
- 3 cloves
- 1 cardamom pod
- 1 black cardamom pod (optional)
- 1 tablespoon coriander seeds
- 1 tablespoon salt
- 1-2 tablespoons fish sauce
- 1-2 tablespoons sugar
- Water

For the Soup:

- Rice noodles (banh pho), prepared according to package instructions
- Thinly sliced beef (sirloin or eye of round)
- Bean sprouts
- Fresh herbs (cilantro, basil, mint)
- Lime wedges
- Chili slices (optional)
- Hoisin sauce and Sriracha, for serving

Instructions:

Char the onions and ginger: Preheat the oven broiler. Place halved onions and sliced ginger on a baking sheet. Broil until they are charred and slightly blackened, about 15-20 minutes.

Parboil the bones: Bring a large pot of water to a boil. Add the beef bones and boil vigorously for 10 minutes. Discard the water and rinse the bones with warm water. Clean the pot.

Simmer the broth: Fill the cleaned pot with about 4 quarts of water. Add the parboiled bones, charred onions, charred ginger, cinnamon stick, star anise, cloves, cardamom pods, black cardamom pod (if using), coriander seeds, salt, fish sauce, and sugar. Bring to a gentle boil.

Skim off the scum: As the broth comes to a boil, use a ladle to skim off any impurities that rise to the surface. Discard the scum.

Simmer the broth: Reduce the heat to low, cover, and let the broth simmer for at least 1.5 to 2 hours. Longer simmering enhances the flavor. Taste and adjust the seasoning with more salt, fish sauce, or sugar as needed.

Prepare the rice noodles: Cook the rice noodles according to the package instructions. Rinse under cold water to stop the cooking process.

Prepare the toppings: Slice the beef thinly. Arrange bean sprouts, fresh herbs, lime wedges, and chili slices on a serving plate.

Assemble the pho: Strain the broth through a fine-mesh strainer to remove solids. Keep the clear broth.

Assemble individual bowls with a portion of rice noodles, sliced beef, and hot broth.

Serve hot: Allow each person to customize their bowl with bean sprouts, fresh herbs, lime wedges, and chili slices. Serve hoisin sauce and Sriracha on the side. Enjoy your homemade Vietnamese Pho!

Note: Pho is all about personal taste, so feel free to adjust the ingredients and toppings according to your preferences.

Cabbage Roll Soup

Ingredients:

- 1 lb ground beef
- 1 onion, finely chopped
- 3 cloves garlic, minced
- 1 small head of cabbage, shredded
- 1 can (28 oz) diced tomatoes
- 1 can (8 oz) tomato sauce
- 4 cups beef broth
- 1 cup cooked rice
- 1 teaspoon dried thyme
- 1 teaspoon paprika
- 1 bay leaf
- Salt and black pepper to taste
- Fresh parsley, chopped, for garnish
- Sour cream, for serving (optional)

Instructions:

In a large pot or Dutch oven, brown the ground beef over medium-high heat. Drain any excess fat.
Add chopped onion to the pot and cook until it becomes translucent, about 5 minutes.
Stir in minced garlic and cook for an additional 1-2 minutes until fragrant.
Add shredded cabbage to the pot and cook until it starts to wilt, about 5 minutes.
Pour in diced tomatoes, tomato sauce, and beef broth. Stir well to combine.
Add cooked rice, dried thyme, paprika, bay leaf, salt, and black pepper. Stir to incorporate the ingredients.
Bring the Cabbage Roll Soup to a simmer. Cover and let it simmer for about 20-30 minutes to allow the flavors to meld.
Adjust the seasoning if needed.
Remove the bay leaf from the soup.
Ladle the soup into bowls.
Garnish with chopped fresh parsley.
Optionally, serve with a dollop of sour cream on top.

Enjoy this hearty and flavorful Cabbage Roll Soup for a comforting and satisfying meal!

Wild Rice and Mushroom Soup

Ingredients:

- 1 cup wild rice, uncooked
- 8 cups vegetable or chicken broth
- 2 tablespoons olive oil
- 1 onion, finely chopped
- 2 carrots, diced
- 2 celery stalks, diced
- 3 cloves garlic, minced
- 8 ounces mushrooms, sliced (button or cremini)
- 1 teaspoon dried thyme
- 1 teaspoon dried rosemary
- 1 bay leaf
- Salt and black pepper to taste
- 1/2 cup all-purpose flour
- 4 cups milk (whole or 2%)
- 1/2 cup heavy cream (optional)
- Fresh parsley, chopped, for garnish

Instructions:

Rinse the wild rice under cold water.
In a large pot, bring the vegetable or chicken broth to a boil. Add the rinsed wild rice, reduce the heat to low, cover, and let it simmer for about 40-45 minutes or until the rice is tender.
In a separate large pot, heat olive oil over medium heat. Add finely chopped onion, diced carrots, diced celery, and minced garlic. Cook until the vegetables are softened, about 5-7 minutes.
Add sliced mushrooms to the pot and cook until they release their moisture and become golden brown.
Stir in dried thyme, dried rosemary, bay leaf, salt, and black pepper.
Sprinkle flour over the mushroom mixture and stir well to create a roux.
Gradually pour in milk, stirring continuously to avoid lumps.
Add the cooked wild rice along with the broth to the pot. Bring the mixture to a simmer.
Optionally, stir in heavy cream for extra richness.
Adjust the seasoning if needed.

Remove the bay leaf from the soup.
Ladle the Wild Rice and Mushroom Soup into bowls.
Garnish with chopped fresh parsley.

Enjoy this wholesome and comforting Wild Rice and Mushroom Soup!

Mexican Pozole

Ingredients:

For the Pozole:

- 2 pounds pork shoulder, cut into bite-sized pieces
- 1 large onion, chopped
- 4 cloves garlic, minced
- 2 cans (29 ounces each) hominy, drained and rinsed
- 1 dried ancho chile
- 1 dried guajillo chile
- 6 cups chicken broth
- 1 teaspoon dried oregano
- 1 teaspoon ground cumin
- Salt and black pepper to taste

For Toppings:

- Shredded cabbage
- Sliced radishes
- Chopped cilantro
- Lime wedges
- Sliced jalapeños
- Diced avocado

Instructions:

In a large pot, combine pork shoulder, chopped onion, minced garlic, hominy, dried ancho chile, dried guajillo chile, chicken broth, dried oregano, ground cumin, salt, and black pepper.
Bring the mixture to a boil, then reduce the heat to low, cover, and let it simmer for about 2 to 2.5 hours or until the pork is tender.
Remove the dried chiles from the pot, and using a blender or food processor, puree them with a little bit of the broth until smooth. Return the puree to the pot.
Continue simmering for an additional 30 minutes to allow the flavors to meld.
Adjust the seasoning if needed.

Ladle the Pozole into bowls.
Serve hot with shredded cabbage, sliced radishes, chopped cilantro, lime wedges, sliced jalapeños, and diced avocado on the side.

Enjoy this traditional and hearty Mexican Pozole!

New England Clam Chowder

Ingredients:

- 4 slices bacon, chopped
- 1 onion, finely chopped
- 2 celery stalks, finely chopped
- 3 tablespoons all-purpose flour
- 3 cups diced potatoes (about 3 medium-sized potatoes)
- 2 cups chicken broth
- 1 cup clam juice (from canned clams)
- 2 cups whole milk
- 1 bay leaf
- 1/2 teaspoon dried thyme
- Salt and black pepper to taste
- 2 cans (6.5 ounces each) chopped clams, drained
- 1 cup heavy cream
- Fresh parsley, chopped, for garnish
- Oyster crackers, for serving (optional)

Instructions:

In a large pot, cook the chopped bacon over medium heat until it becomes crispy. Remove some bacon bits for garnish and leave some in the pot for flavor.
Add finely chopped onion and celery to the pot. Cook until the vegetables are softened, about 5 minutes.
Sprinkle all-purpose flour over the vegetables and bacon in the pot. Stir well to create a roux.
Add diced potatoes, chicken broth, clam juice, whole milk, bay leaf, dried thyme, salt, and black pepper to the pot. Stir to combine.
Bring the mixture to a simmer, then reduce the heat to low, cover, and let it simmer for about 15-20 minutes or until the potatoes are tender.
Stir in the drained chopped clams and heavy cream. Simmer for an additional 5-7 minutes until heated through.
Adjust the seasoning if needed.
Remove the bay leaf from the chowder.
Ladle the New England Clam Chowder into bowls.
Garnish with the reserved crispy bacon bits and chopped fresh parsley.
Optionally, serve with oyster crackers on the side.

Enjoy this creamy and flavorful New England Clam Chowder for a comforting and satisfying meal!

Lemon Chicken Orzo Soup

Ingredients:

- 1 tablespoon olive oil
- 1 onion, finely chopped
- 2 carrots, diced
- 2 celery stalks, diced
- 3 cloves garlic, minced
- 6 cups chicken broth
- 1 cup cooked shredded chicken
- 1/2 cup uncooked orzo pasta
- 2 eggs
- Juice of 2 lemons
- Zest of 1 lemon
- Salt and black pepper to taste
- Fresh dill, chopped, for garnish

Instructions:

In a large pot, heat olive oil over medium heat. Add finely chopped onion, diced carrots, diced celery, and minced garlic. Cook until the vegetables are softened, about 5 minutes.
Pour in chicken broth and bring the mixture to a simmer.
Add cooked shredded chicken and uncooked orzo pasta to the pot. Simmer for about 10-12 minutes or until the orzo is cooked al dente.
In a bowl, whisk together eggs, lemon juice, and lemon zest.
Gradually whisk a ladleful of hot broth into the egg-lemon mixture to temper it.
This prevents the eggs from curdling when added to the soup.
Slowly pour the egg-lemon mixture back into the pot while stirring constantly.
Continue stirring for a few minutes until the soup thickens slightly.
Season the Lemon Chicken Orzo Soup with salt and black pepper to taste.
Adjust the seasoning if needed.
Ladle the soup into bowls.
Garnish with chopped fresh dill.

Enjoy this comforting and citrusy Lemon Chicken Orzo Soup!

Cucumber Avocado Soup

Ingredients:

- 2 large cucumbers, peeled and chopped
- 2 ripe avocados, peeled and pitted
- 1 cup plain Greek yogurt
- 1/4 cup fresh cilantro, chopped
- 2 tablespoons fresh mint, chopped
- 2 tablespoons lime juice
- 1 clove garlic, minced
- 2 cups vegetable broth
- Salt and black pepper to taste
- Optional toppings: diced cucumber, avocado slices, drizzle of olive oil, and additional herbs for garnish

Instructions:

In a blender or food processor, combine chopped cucumbers, peeled and pitted avocados, Greek yogurt, fresh cilantro, fresh mint, lime juice, minced garlic, and vegetable broth.
Blend until smooth and creamy.
Season the Cucumber Avocado Soup with salt and black pepper to taste. Adjust the seasoning if needed.
Chill the soup in the refrigerator for at least 2 hours before serving.
Before serving, give the soup a good stir. If it has thickened too much, you can add a bit more vegetable broth to reach your desired consistency.
Ladle the soup into bowls.
Garnish with diced cucumber, avocado slices, a drizzle of olive oil, and additional chopped herbs if desired.
Serve chilled and enjoy this cool and creamy Cucumber Avocado Soup!

This soup is perfect for a light and refreshing meal, especially on warm days.

Black-Eyed Pea Soup

Ingredients:

- 1 cup dried black-eyed peas, soaked overnight and drained
- 1 tablespoon olive oil
- 1 onion, chopped
- 2 carrots, diced
- 2 celery stalks, diced
- 3 cloves garlic, minced
- 1 ham hock or smoked turkey leg (optional, for flavor)
- 6 cups chicken or vegetable broth
- 1 can (14 ounces) diced tomatoes, undrained
- 1 teaspoon dried thyme
- 1 teaspoon smoked paprika
- 1 bay leaf
- Salt and black pepper to taste
- 4 cups chopped fresh spinach or kale
- Lemon wedges, for serving

Instructions:

In a large pot, heat olive oil over medium heat. Add chopped onion, diced carrots, diced celery, and minced garlic. Cook until the vegetables are softened, about 5 minutes.
Add soaked and drained black-eyed peas to the pot.
If using, add a ham hock or smoked turkey leg to the pot for additional flavor.
Pour in chicken or vegetable broth, diced tomatoes with their juice, dried thyme, smoked paprika, bay leaf, salt, and black pepper. Stir to combine.
Bring the mixture to a boil, then reduce the heat to low, cover, and let it simmer for about 45 minutes to 1 hour or until the black-eyed peas are tender.
Remove the ham hock or smoked turkey leg from the pot. If using, shred the meat and return it to the soup.
Stir in chopped fresh spinach or kale and let it wilt in the hot soup.
Adjust the seasoning if needed.
Remove the bay leaf from the soup.
Ladle the Black-Eyed Pea Soup into bowls.
Serve hot with lemon wedges on the side.

Enjoy this nutritious and hearty Black-Eyed Pea Soup, which is often associated with good luck in many cultures!

Italian Sausage and Bean Soup

Ingredients:

- 1 cup dried black-eyed peas, soaked overnight and drained
- 1 tablespoon olive oil
- 1 onion, chopped
- 2 carrots, diced
- 2 celery stalks, diced
- 3 cloves garlic, minced
- 1 ham hock or smoked turkey leg (optional, for flavor)
- 6 cups chicken or vegetable broth
- 1 can (14 ounces) diced tomatoes, undrained
- 1 teaspoon dried thyme
- 1 teaspoon smoked paprika
- 1 bay leaf
- Salt and black pepper to taste
- 4 cups chopped fresh spinach or kale
- Lemon wedges, for serving

Instructions:

In a large pot, heat olive oil over medium heat. Add chopped onion, diced carrots, diced celery, and minced garlic. Cook until the vegetables are softened, about 5 minutes.
Add soaked and drained black-eyed peas to the pot.
If using, add a ham hock or smoked turkey leg to the pot for additional flavor.
Pour in chicken or vegetable broth, diced tomatoes with their juice, dried thyme, smoked paprika, bay leaf, salt, and black pepper. Stir to combine.
Bring the mixture to a boil, then reduce the heat to low, cover, and let it simmer for about 45 minutes to 1 hour or until the black-eyed peas are tender.
Remove the ham hock or smoked turkey leg from the pot. If using, shred the meat and return it to the soup.
Stir in chopped fresh spinach or kale and let it wilt in the hot soup.
Adjust the seasoning if needed.
Remove the bay leaf from the soup.
Ladle the Black-Eyed Pea Soup into bowls.
Serve hot with lemon wedges on the side.

Enjoy this nutritious and hearty Black-Eyed Pea Soup, which is often associated with good luck in many cultures!

Pistou Soup

Ingredients:

For the Soup:

- 2 tablespoons olive oil
- 1 onion, chopped
- 2 carrots, diced
- 2 celery stalks, diced
- 3 cloves garlic, minced
- 1 can (14 ounces) diced tomatoes, undrained
- 6 cups vegetable broth
- 1 can (14 ounces) cannellini beans, drained and rinsed
- 1 cup green beans, trimmed and cut into bite-sized pieces
- 1 cup small pasta (such as ditalini or small elbow pasta)
- Salt and black pepper to taste

For the Pistou:

- 2 cups fresh basil leaves
- 3 cloves garlic
- 1/2 cup grated Parmesan cheese
- 1/2 cup extra-virgin olive oil
- Salt to taste

Instructions:

For the Soup:

In a large pot, heat olive oil over medium heat. Add chopped onion, diced carrots, diced celery, and minced garlic. Cook until the vegetables are softened, about 5 minutes.

Add diced tomatoes with their juice, vegetable broth, cannellini beans, green beans, and pasta to the pot. Stir to combine.

Bring the mixture to a boil, then reduce the heat to low, cover, and let it simmer for about 15-20 minutes or until the pasta is cooked and the vegetables are tender.

Season the soup with salt and black pepper to taste.
Adjust the seasoning if needed.

For the Pistou:

In a food processor, combine fresh basil leaves, garlic, grated Parmesan cheese, and salt.
Pulse until the ingredients are finely chopped.
With the food processor running, slowly drizzle in the extra-virgin olive oil until the mixture becomes a smooth paste.

To Serve:

Ladle the Pistou Soup into bowls.
Swirl a spoonful of pistou on top of each bowl of soup.
Serve hot and enjoy this flavorful and aromatic Pistou Soup!

Pistou is a Provençal cold sauce similar to pesto, and when added to the hot soup, it provides a burst of fresh flavors.

Chicken and Corn Chowder

Ingredients:

- 1 tablespoon olive oil
- 1 onion, diced
- 2 carrots, diced
- 2 celery stalks, diced
- 3 cloves garlic, minced
- 1 pound boneless, skinless chicken breasts, cooked and shredded
- 3 cups corn kernels (fresh or frozen)
- 3 cups diced potatoes
- 4 cups chicken broth
- 2 cups milk
- 1 cup heavy cream
- 1 teaspoon dried thyme
- 1 teaspoon smoked paprika
- Salt and black pepper to taste
- 1/4 cup all-purpose flour (for thickening, if desired)
- Fresh parsley, chopped, for garnish

Instructions:

In a large pot, heat olive oil over medium heat. Add diced onion, diced carrots, diced celery, and minced garlic. Cook until the vegetables are softened, about 5 minutes.

Add shredded cooked chicken, corn kernels, diced potatoes, chicken broth, milk, heavy cream, dried thyme, smoked paprika, salt, and black pepper to the pot. Stir to combine.

Bring the mixture to a boil, then reduce the heat to low, cover, and let it simmer for about 15-20 minutes or until the potatoes are tender.

If you prefer a thicker chowder, you can mix 1/4 cup of all-purpose flour with a little water to create a slurry. Stir the slurry into the chowder and simmer for an additional 5-7 minutes until it thickens.

Adjust the seasoning if needed.

Ladle the Chicken and Corn Chowder into bowls.

Garnish with chopped fresh parsley.

Serve hot and enjoy this creamy and comforting chowder!

This Chicken and Corn Chowder is a hearty and satisfying soup that's perfect for a comforting meal.

White Gazpacho

Ingredients:

- 2 cups blanched almonds, peeled
- 4 cups seedless green grapes, plus extra for garnish
- 2 cucumbers, peeled and chopped
- 2 cloves garlic, minced
- 3 cups white bread, crust removed, cubed
- 4 cups cold vegetable broth
- 1/4 cup white wine vinegar
- 1/2 cup extra-virgin olive oil
- Salt and white pepper to taste
- Fresh mint leaves, for garnish
- Sliced almonds, toasted, for garnish

Instructions:

In a blender or food processor, combine blanched almonds, seedless green grapes, chopped cucumbers, minced garlic, and white bread cubes.
Blend the ingredients until you have a smooth puree.
With the blender or food processor running, slowly drizzle in the white wine vinegar and extra-virgin olive oil until the mixture is well combined.
Gradually add the cold vegetable broth while continuing to blend until the gazpacho reaches a silky consistency.
Season the White Gazpacho with salt and white pepper to taste. Adjust the seasoning if needed.
Chill the gazpacho in the refrigerator for at least 2 hours before serving.
Before serving, give the gazpacho a good stir. If it has thickened too much, you can add a bit more cold vegetable broth to reach your desired consistency.
Ladle the White Gazpacho into bowls.
Garnish each bowl with additional seedless green grapes, fresh mint leaves, and toasted sliced almonds.
Serve chilled and enjoy this unique and refreshing White Gazpacho!

This cold soup is perfect for warm days and showcases the delightful combination of almonds, grapes, and cucumbers.

Zuppa Toscana

Ingredients:

- 1 pound Italian sausage (spicy or mild), casings removed
- 1 large onion, finely chopped
- 3 cloves garlic, minced
- 4 cups russet potatoes, peeled and sliced into thin rounds
- 4 cups kale, stems removed and chopped
- 6 cups chicken broth
- 1 cup heavy cream
- Salt and black pepper to taste
- 1/2 teaspoon red pepper flakes (optional, for extra heat)
- Grated Parmesan cheese, for serving

Instructions:

In a large pot, brown the Italian sausage over medium heat, breaking it into crumbles as it cooks. Once fully cooked, remove any excess fat.
Add finely chopped onion to the pot and cook until it becomes translucent, about 5 minutes.
Stir in minced garlic and cook for an additional 1-2 minutes until fragrant.
Add sliced potatoes to the pot and pour in chicken broth. Bring the mixture to a simmer and let it cook until the potatoes are tender, about 15-20 minutes.
Once the potatoes are cooked, add chopped kale to the pot. Cook for an additional 5 minutes until the kale is wilted.
Pour in heavy cream and season the Zuppa Toscana with salt, black pepper, and red pepper flakes (if using). Stir well to combine.
Simmer the soup for an additional 5-10 minutes to allow the flavors to meld.
Taste and adjust the seasoning if needed.
Ladle the Zuppa Toscana into bowls.
Optionally, garnish each bowl with grated Parmesan cheese.
Serve hot and enjoy this comforting and flavorful Italian soup!

Zuppa Toscana is known for its hearty combination of sausage, potatoes, and kale in a creamy broth, making it a perfect and satisfying dish.

Turkey and Wild Rice Soup

Ingredients:

- 1 cup wild rice, uncooked
- 2 tablespoons olive oil
- 1 onion, finely chopped
- 2 carrots, diced
- 2 celery stalks, diced
- 3 cloves garlic, minced
- 4 cups shredded cooked turkey (or chicken)
- 8 cups chicken or turkey broth
- 1 teaspoon dried thyme
- 1 teaspoon dried sage
- Salt and black pepper to taste
- 1 cup mushrooms, sliced
- 1/2 cup all-purpose flour
- 1 cup milk
- 1 cup heavy cream
- Fresh parsley, chopped, for garnish

Instructions:

Cook the wild rice according to package instructions. Set aside.
In a large pot, heat olive oil over medium heat. Add finely chopped onion, diced carrots, diced celery, and minced garlic. Cook until the vegetables are softened, about 5 minutes.
Add shredded cooked turkey to the pot.
Pour in chicken or turkey broth, dried thyme, dried sage, salt, and black pepper. Stir to combine.
Bring the mixture to a simmer, then reduce the heat to low, cover, and let it simmer for about 15-20 minutes.
Add sliced mushrooms to the pot and continue simmering for an additional 5-7 minutes until the mushrooms are cooked.
In a separate bowl, whisk together all-purpose flour and milk until smooth. Gradually whisk the flour-milk mixture into the soup to thicken it. Stir continuously to avoid lumps.
Pour in heavy cream and cooked wild rice. Stir well to combine.

Adjust the seasoning if needed.
Simmer the Turkey and Wild Rice Soup for an additional 10 minutes to allow the flavors to meld.
Ladle the soup into bowls.
Garnish with chopped fresh parsley.
Serve hot and enjoy this comforting and hearty Turkey and Wild Rice Soup!

This soup is a great way to use leftover turkey and combines the earthy flavor of wild rice with a creamy broth.

Spicy Pumpkin Soup

Ingredients:

- 2 tablespoons olive oil
- 1 onion, chopped
- 3 cloves garlic, minced
- 1 teaspoon ground cumin
- 1/2 teaspoon ground coriander
- 1/2 teaspoon smoked paprika
- 1/4 teaspoon cayenne pepper (adjust to taste)
- 4 cups pumpkin puree (canned or homemade)
- 4 cups vegetable broth
- 1 can (14 ounces) coconut milk
- Salt and black pepper to taste
- 1 tablespoon maple syrup (optional, for sweetness)
- Greek yogurt or sour cream, for garnish
- Pumpkin seeds, toasted, for garnish
- Fresh cilantro or parsley, chopped, for garnish

Instructions:

In a large pot, heat olive oil over medium heat. Add chopped onion and cook until it becomes translucent, about 5 minutes.
Stir in minced garlic, ground cumin, ground coriander, smoked paprika, and cayenne pepper. Cook for an additional 2 minutes until the spices are fragrant.
Add pumpkin puree, vegetable broth, and coconut milk to the pot. Stir well to combine.
Bring the mixture to a simmer, then reduce the heat to low, cover, and let it simmer for about 15-20 minutes to allow the flavors to meld.
Season the Spicy Pumpkin Soup with salt and black pepper to taste. Adjust the seasoning if needed.
If you prefer a touch of sweetness, stir in maple syrup.
Using an immersion blender, blend the soup until smooth. Alternatively, transfer the soup to a blender and blend in batches, being careful as the soup will be hot.
Ladle the soup into bowls.
Garnish each bowl with a dollop of Greek yogurt or sour cream, toasted pumpkin seeds, and chopped fresh cilantro or parsley.

Serve hot and enjoy this Spicy Pumpkin Soup with a kick!

This soup is perfect for the fall season, and the combination of pumpkin and spices creates a warming and flavorful dish.

Artichoke Soup

Ingredients:

- 2 tablespoons olive oil
- 1 onion, chopped
- 2 cloves garlic, minced
- 2 cans (14 ounces each) artichoke hearts, drained and chopped
- 1 large potato, peeled and diced
- 4 cups vegetable broth
- 1 cup milk (or substitute with almond or soy milk for a dairy-free option)
- 1/2 cup heavy cream (optional, for added richness)
- 1 teaspoon dried thyme
- Salt and black pepper to taste
- 1/4 cup grated Parmesan cheese (optional, for garnish)
- Fresh chives, chopped, for garnish

Instructions:

In a large pot, heat olive oil over medium heat. Add chopped onion and cook until it becomes translucent, about 5 minutes.
Stir in minced garlic and cook for an additional 1-2 minutes until fragrant.
Add chopped artichoke hearts and diced potato to the pot. Cook for 3-5 minutes, allowing the ingredients to meld.
Pour in vegetable broth and bring the mixture to a simmer. Cook until the potatoes are tender, about 15-20 minutes.
Using an immersion blender, blend the soup until smooth. Alternatively, transfer the soup to a blender and blend in batches, being careful as the soup will be hot.
Return the blended soup to the pot and place it back on the heat.
Stir in milk and, if using, heavy cream for added richness.
Season the Artichoke Soup with dried thyme, salt, and black pepper. Adjust the seasoning if needed.
Ladle the soup into bowls.
Optionally, garnish each bowl with grated Parmesan cheese and chopped fresh chives.
Serve hot and enjoy this creamy and flavorful Artichoke Soup!

This soup showcases the rich and unique flavor of artichokes, creating a delightful and comforting dish.

Chicken Mulligatawny Soup

Ingredients:

- 2 tablespoons vegetable oil
- 1 onion, finely chopped
- 2 carrots, diced
- 2 celery stalks, diced
- 3 cloves garlic, minced
- 1 tablespoon curry powder
- 1 teaspoon ground cumin
- 1 teaspoon ground coriander
- 1/2 teaspoon turmeric
- 1/4 teaspoon cayenne pepper (adjust to taste)
- 1 cup red lentils, rinsed and drained
- 1 pound boneless, skinless chicken breasts, cut into bite-sized pieces
- 6 cups chicken broth
- 1 can (14 ounces) diced tomatoes, undrained
- 1/2 cup apple, peeled and diced
- 1/2 cup coconut milk
- Salt and black pepper to taste
- Fresh cilantro, chopped, for garnish
- Lemon wedges, for serving

Instructions:

In a large pot, heat vegetable oil over medium heat. Add finely chopped onion, diced carrots, diced celery, and minced garlic. Cook until the vegetables are softened, about 5 minutes.

Stir in curry powder, ground cumin, ground coriander, turmeric, and cayenne pepper. Cook for an additional 2 minutes until the spices are fragrant.

Add red lentils, chicken pieces, chicken broth, diced tomatoes, diced apple, and coconut milk to the pot. Stir well to combine.

Bring the mixture to a boil, then reduce the heat to low, cover, and let it simmer for about 20-25 minutes or until the lentils are cooked and the chicken is tender.

Season the Chicken Mulligatawny Soup with salt and black pepper to taste.

Adjust the seasoning if needed.

Ladle the soup into bowls.

Garnish each bowl with chopped fresh cilantro.

Serve hot with lemon wedges on the side for squeezing.
Enjoy this flavorful and spiced Chicken Mulligatawny Soup!

Mulligatawny Soup is a fusion of Indian and British cuisine, known for its rich and aromatic flavor profile.

Chickpea and Spinach Soup

Ingredients:

- 2 tablespoons olive oil
- 1 onion, finely chopped
- 2 carrots, diced
- 2 celery stalks, diced
- 3 cloves garlic, minced
- 1 teaspoon ground cumin
- 1 teaspoon ground coriander
- 1/2 teaspoon smoked paprika
- 1 can (15 ounces) chickpeas, drained and rinsed
- 4 cups vegetable broth
- 1 can (14 ounces) diced tomatoes, undrained
- 1 bay leaf
- 1 cup small pasta (such as ditalini or small shells)
- 4 cups fresh spinach, chopped
- Salt and black pepper to taste
- Fresh lemon juice, for serving
- Grated Parmesan cheese, for serving (optional)

Instructions:

In a large pot, heat olive oil over medium heat. Add finely chopped onion, diced carrots, diced celery, and minced garlic. Cook until the vegetables are softened, about 5 minutes.

Stir in ground cumin, ground coriander, and smoked paprika. Cook for an additional 2 minutes until the spices are fragrant.

Add chickpeas, vegetable broth, diced tomatoes, and bay leaf to the pot. Stir well to combine.

Bring the mixture to a boil, then reduce the heat to low, cover, and let it simmer for about 15-20 minutes.

Meanwhile, cook the small pasta according to package instructions. Drain and set aside.

Once the soup has simmered, add the cooked pasta and chopped fresh spinach to the pot. Stir until the spinach wilts and the pasta is heated through.

Season the Chickpea and Spinach Soup with salt and black pepper to taste.
Adjust the seasoning if needed.
Remove the bay leaf from the soup.
Ladle the soup into bowls.
Optionally, squeeze fresh lemon juice over each serving and garnish with grated Parmesan cheese.
Serve hot and enjoy this nutritious and satisfying Chickpea and Spinach Soup!

This soup is a hearty and flavorful dish that combines the protein-rich chickpeas with the freshness of spinach, creating a wholesome meal.

Smoky Lentil Soup

Ingredients:

- 2 tablespoons olive oil
- 1 onion, finely chopped
- 2 carrots, diced
- 2 celery stalks, diced
- 3 cloves garlic, minced
- 1 teaspoon smoked paprika
- 1 teaspoon ground cumin
- 1/2 teaspoon ground coriander
- 1 cup dried green or brown lentils, rinsed and drained
- 1 can (14 ounces) diced tomatoes, undrained
- 6 cups vegetable broth
- 2 bay leaves
- 1 teaspoon liquid smoke (optional, for extra smokiness)
- Salt and black pepper to taste
- Fresh parsley, chopped, for garnish
- Lemon wedges, for serving

Instructions:

In a large pot, heat olive oil over medium heat. Add finely chopped onion, diced carrots, diced celery, and minced garlic. Cook until the vegetables are softened, about 5 minutes.

Stir in smoked paprika, ground cumin, and ground coriander. Cook for an additional 2 minutes until the spices are fragrant.

Add rinsed lentils, diced tomatoes with their juice, vegetable broth, bay leaves, and liquid smoke (if using) to the pot. Stir well to combine.

Bring the mixture to a boil, then reduce the heat to low, cover, and let it simmer for about 25-30 minutes or until the lentils are tender.

Season the Smoky Lentil Soup with salt and black pepper to taste. Adjust the seasoning if needed.

Remove the bay leaves from the soup.

Ladle the soup into bowls.

Garnish each bowl with chopped fresh parsley.

Serve hot with lemon wedges on the side for squeezing.

Enjoy this hearty and smoky Lentil Soup!

The addition of smoked paprika and liquid smoke gives this lentil soup a rich and smoky flavor, making it a comforting and satisfying dish.

Creamy Asparagus Soup

Ingredients:

- 2 tablespoons unsalted butter
- 1 onion, chopped
- 2 pounds asparagus, tough ends trimmed and spears chopped
- 3 cups vegetable broth
- 1 potato, peeled and diced
- 2 cups milk
- Salt and white pepper to taste
- 1/2 cup heavy cream
- Lemon zest, for garnish
- Fresh chives, chopped, for garnish

Instructions:

In a large pot, melt the butter over medium heat. Add the chopped onion and cook until it becomes translucent, about 5 minutes.
Add the chopped asparagus spears to the pot, reserving a few tips for garnish. Cook for an additional 5 minutes, stirring occasionally.
Pour in the vegetable broth and add the diced potato. Bring the mixture to a boil, then reduce the heat to low, cover, and let it simmer for about 15-20 minutes or until the asparagus and potato are tender.
Using an immersion blender, blend the soup until smooth. Alternatively, transfer the soup to a blender and blend in batches, being careful as the soup will be hot. Return the blended soup to the pot and place it back on the heat.
Stir in the milk and season the soup with salt and white pepper to taste. Adjust the seasoning if needed.
Add the heavy cream and stir well to combine.
In a separate pan, blanch the reserved asparagus tips in boiling water for 2-3 minutes until they are bright green and slightly tender. Drain and set aside.
Ladle the Creamy Asparagus Soup into bowls.
Garnish each bowl with lemon zest, chopped fresh chives, and the blanched asparagus tips.
Serve hot and enjoy this velvety and flavorful Creamy Asparagus Soup!

This soup celebrates the delicate and fresh flavor of asparagus, creating a creamy and comforting dish.

Beef Pho

Ingredients:

For the Broth:

- 2 large onions, halved (unpeeled)
- 1 large piece of ginger (about 3 inches), halved lengthwise
- 3-4 lbs beef bones (marrow and knuckle bones)
- 1 lb beef brisket or flank steak
- 1 cinnamon stick
- 3 star anise
- 3 cloves
- 1 cardamom pod
- 1 tablespoon coriander seeds
- 1 tablespoon salt
- 2 tablespoons fish sauce
- 1 tablespoon sugar
- 1 onion, thinly sliced (for serving)
- Fresh cilantro, basil, bean sprouts, lime wedges (for serving)

For the Noodles and Toppings:

- Rice noodles (banh pho), cooked according to package instructions
- Thinly sliced beef (flank steak or sirloin), cooked in the hot broth
- Fresh cilantro, basil leaves, and bean sprouts (for garnish)
- Lime wedges, sliced chili, and hoisin sauce (for serving)

Instructions:

Char the onions and ginger: Preheat the broiler. Place the onion halves and ginger on a baking sheet and char under the broiler for about 15-20 minutes, turning occasionally. The goal is to get a nice char on the skins.

Parboil the beef bones: Bring a large pot of water to a boil. Add the beef bones and boil vigorously for 10 minutes. Discard the water, clean the bones, and rinse the pot.

Simmer the broth: Fill the pot with about 4 quarts of water. Add the parboiled bones, charred onions, ginger, cinnamon stick, star anise, cloves, cardamom pod, coriander seeds, salt, fish sauce, and sugar. Bring to a boil, then reduce the heat to low. Let it simmer gently for 1.5 to 2 hours, skimming the surface to remove any impurities.

Prepare the beef: Slice the beef brisket or flank steak into thin slices. You can briefly blanch the slices in the hot broth before serving.

Strain the broth: After simmering, strain the broth through a fine-mesh strainer. Adjust the seasoning with more fish sauce or salt if needed.

Assemble the bowls: Cook the rice noodles according to the package instructions. Place a handful of cooked noodles into each serving bowl. Top with the sliced beef.

Pour the hot broth: Ladle the hot broth over the noodles and beef. The hot broth will cook the raw beef slices.

Serve with toppings: Add thinly sliced onions, fresh cilantro, basil leaves, and bean sprouts to each bowl. Serve with lime wedges, sliced chili, and hoisin sauce on the side.

Enjoy your homemade Beef Pho!

This recipe allows you to create a rich and flavorful beef pho broth at home, providing a comforting and delicious Vietnamese noodle soup experience.

Lemon Dill Chicken Soup

Ingredients:

- 2 tablespoons olive oil
- 1 onion, finely chopped
- 2 carrots, diced
- 2 celery stalks, diced
- 3 cloves garlic, minced
- 6 cups chicken broth
- 1 pound boneless, skinless chicken breasts, cooked and shredded
- 1/2 cup orzo pasta (or rice)
- Juice of 2 lemons
- Zest of 1 lemon
- 2 teaspoons dried dill
- Salt and black pepper to taste
- Fresh dill, chopped, for garnish
- Lemon slices, for garnish

Instructions:

In a large pot, heat olive oil over medium heat. Add finely chopped onion, diced carrots, diced celery, and minced garlic. Cook until the vegetables are softened, about 5 minutes.
Pour in the chicken broth and bring the mixture to a simmer.
Add shredded cooked chicken to the pot.
Stir in orzo pasta (or rice) and cook until the pasta is al dente or the rice is cooked according to package instructions.
Add the juice of 2 lemons, lemon zest, and dried dill to the soup. Stir well to combine.
Season the Lemon Dill Chicken Soup with salt and black pepper to taste. Adjust the seasoning if needed.
Let the soup simmer for an additional 5-10 minutes to allow the flavors to meld.
Ladle the soup into bowls.
Garnish each bowl with chopped fresh dill and lemon slices.
Serve hot and enjoy this bright and flavorful Lemon Dill Chicken Soup!

This soup is a refreshing twist on traditional chicken soup, with the bright flavors of lemon and dill adding a delightful touch.